PRACTICING THE JHĀNAS

*To the Venerable Pa Auk Sayadaw
with gratitude and respect*

PRACTICING THE
Jhānas

*Traditional Concentration
Meditation as Presented by the*
Venerable Pa Auk Sayadaw

STEPHEN SNYDER AND
TINA RASMUSSEN

SHAMBHALA
Boston & London
2009

Shambhala Publications, Inc.
Horticultural Hall
300 Massachusetts Avenue
Boston, Massachusetts 02115
www.shambhala.com

9 8 7 6 5 4

Printed in the United States of America

♾ This edition is printed on acid-free paper that meets the
American National Standards Institute z39.48 Standard.
♻ Shambhala Publications makes every effort to print on recycled paper.
For more information please visit www.shambhala.com.
Distributed in the United States by Random House, Inc.,
and in Canada by Random House of Canada Ltd

Designed by Steve Dyer

Library of Congress Cataloging-in-Publication Data
Snyder, Stephen, 1957–
Practicing the jhanas/Stephen Snyder and Tina Rasmussen.—1st ed.
p. cm.
Includes bibliographical references and index.
ISBN 978-1-59030-733-5 (pbk.: alk. paper)
1. Samatha (Buddhism) I. Rasmussen, Tina. II. Title.
BQ5612.S62 2009
294.3′4435—dc22
2009017722

Contents

Foreword

THIS BOOK SERVES as a bridge—as a conduit to the traditional teachings of the Buddha that are outlined in the suttas, the *Visuddhimagga,* and my book *Knowing and Seeing.* My wish is that more practitioners will apply these suggestions in order to attain *jhāna* and go on to complete the entire Buddhist path. Obtaining and applying the concentration of the jhānas allows the student to progress more quickly and deeply through the *vipassanā* portion of the Buddhist path. The jhāna practice itself, however, has its own inherent value as a path of purification, the same one undertaken by the Buddha himself.

Many years ago, my teacher told me to plant the seed of this teaching in the West. This book serves to water this seed and help it flower. I wholeheartedly recommend it to all who are drawn to the jhānas and to all who seek to practice the Buddhist path as the Buddha lived and taught it.

Stephen Snyder and Tina Rasmussen (Ayya Pesala) know what they write about in this book, personally, through their own direct experience as practitioners and dedicated yogis. Both of them worked diligently under my direct guidance to attain mastery of the eight jhānas and the additional meditation practices.

—PA AUK SAYADAW

Preface

FOR NEARLY twenty-six hundred years, Buddhist meditation masters have painstakingly preserved the rich meditation practice of absorption concentration called jhāna. We are fortunate to have a modern jhāna master—the Venerable Pa Auk Sayadaw—who through his books and retreats has made the Buddha's teachings more accessible to meditators both within his native country of Myanmar (Burma) and around the world.

In 2005, we undertook a two-month jhāna retreat with the Venerable Pa Auk Sayadaw in Middletown, California. This book is an offering of our experiences with the *samatha* practice, as we learned it under the direct and personal guidance of the Venerable Pa Auk Sayadaw. We are not Buddhist scholars or historians and have written this book based on our direct experience as dedicated practitioners.

This book is designed to be used in conjunction with the Sayadaw's book *Knowing and Seeing,* which is an excellent reference that details all three aspects of Buddhist practice: *sīla,* samatha, and vipassanā. We also encourage you to read the suttas and the *Visuddhimagga* yourself.

In this book, we focus primarily on the samatha portion of the path. Our intent is to, in some small way, bridge the gap between the traditional Buddhist teachings and the conceptual and practical understanding of concentration meditation shared by modern practitioners. For those drawn to this exquisite practice and this book, we wish you many blessings on your path of purification.

Acknowledgments

FIRST AND FOREMOST, we want to thank Robert Cusick. Without him, this book would not have come into being. Robert, thank you for going to Burma and facing the challenges you encountered there so you could bring your enthusiasm for this practice back to share with others. Thank you for introducing us to each other. You may never have thought we'd thank you for "encouraging" us (strongly) to write this book, but we are eternally grateful.

Roland Win was also a huge contributor to this book's coming to fruition. His sponsorship enabled the Venerable Pa Auk Sayadaw to teach the Four Springs Retreat. And he hand-carried the first draft of the manuscript for this book to Sri Lanka himself so that the Sayadaw could personally review it.

Many thanks to Guy Armstrong for his insight and encouragement. Guy was one of the first reviewers of the manuscript and also introduced Tina to jhāna practice.

We would also like to express our gratitude to the following people who also reviewed the manuscript and gave us valuable feedback: Rick Hanson, Michael Hagerty, Cyndia Biver, Gil Fronsdal, and Bhante U Jagara.

Thanks also to Gil for his support and guidance as we move into the role of supporting others in this practice.

A special thanks to Shambhala Publications for publishing this book. We are deeply appreciative of our editor, Emily Bower, for her enthusiasm for our book, her unfailing focus on improving the book for the reader, and her clear love of Buddhism and respect for these traditional Theravadin Buddhist practices.

Finally, we would like to thank the many meditators from around the world who have taken up this practice, asked great questions, and inspired us to teach.

1

History of the Jhānas

WHEN THE BODHISATTVA Siddhārtha could no longer resist the inner call of liberation, he left behind his family and the luxury of palace life. Shaving off his hair and beard, he donned the robes of a *samana*—a wandering religious seeker. He went to study with the few select teachers of his day who were accomplished in the concentration practices of *jhāna,* which led to purification of mind. First, Siddhārtha went to Alara Kalama, from whom he learned the first material jhāna through the seventh immaterial jhāna (the base of nothingness). Despite these attainments, Siddhārtha continued his pursuit and sought out Uddaka Ramaputta to learn and practice the highest attainment of the day—the eighth immaterial jhāna (the base of neither perception nor nonperception). Completing these attainments was the foundation for the bodhisattva's path to eventual Buddhahood.[1]

Over the next forty years, the Buddha gave many public talks, or "suttas," which were memorized and orally transmitted from monastic to monastic for hundreds of years. The suttas were then transcribed into writing as the Pāli Canon. In many suttas, the

Buddha repeatedly encourages seekers of liberation to take up the practice of jhāna. A few hundred years later, Bhadantacariya Buddhagosa compiled a detailed meditation manual entitled the *Visuddhimagga*[2] (The Path of Purification), which describes the specifics of many forms of Buddhist meditation practice, including the jhānas.

The story of the jhānas is a long one, so ancient that it predates written history and even Buddhism itself. It is worth knowing, if for no other reason than to demonstrate the durability of this practice over the millennia and its worthiness to remain as a pillar of our modern Buddhist practices—not as a supplemental or side practice, or something done for fun or for blissful spiritual experiences, but because it has been done through the ages as a foundational method for purifying the mind.

As in the old days, many modern Buddhists feel drawn to emulate the meditative path of the Buddha himself. Those of us who see the Buddha not only as a cherished icon but also as an actual role model for how we should practice can harbor very little doubt that concentration meditation in the pursuit of jhāna is warranted. Some people believe that the demanding requirements of practicing the jhānas according to the suttas and the *Visuddhimagga* make it a lofty goal, beyond actual reach. You may even believe that it is unlikely, if not impossible, to attain the jhānas as described in the instructions outlined in the *Visuddhimagga*. Fortunately, we have in our time a meditation master—in the person of the Venerable Pa Auk Sayadaw—whose voluminous books on the Buddha's path over his long and distinguished career have made these once obscure teachings more accessible. We believe that with his traditional presentation and the historical basis for jhāna practice, coupled with firsthand experiential pointers, modern practitioners can undertake this rigorous form of concentration practice and indeed make progress in the purification of mind.

· · ·

For us, one of the primary reasons for undertaking concentration practice was the Buddha's own path. In reading a broad selection of the suttas, you will find that the Buddha mentions jhāna over and over. Why was it so important to him? We wanted to find out for ourselves, as do an increasing number of meditators today.

At the time of the Buddha, nearly twenty-six hundred years ago, jhāna practice was widespread. The young prince Siddhārtha first experienced jhāna when meditating as a young boy. "I recall once when my father the Shakyan was working, and I was sitting in the cool shade of a rose-apple tree, then quite withdrawn from sensuality, withdrawn from unskillful mental qualities—I entered and remained in the first jhāna."[3]

When Siddhārtha undertook the ascetic life in search of spiritual awakening, one of the first practices in which he engaged was concentration meditation and the rigorous practice of the jhānas.[4] Throughout his long life, the Buddha cited *samatha* practice extensively as an essential part of the path of practice. In fact, entering jhāna was not only the Buddha's final meditative practice but also the final action of his life:

> Then the Blessed One addressed the monks, "Now then, [monastics], I exhort you: All fabrications are subject to decay. Bring about completion by being heedful." Those were the Tathagata's last words. Then the Blessed One entered the first jhāna.[5]

His final action was to enter each of the jhānas sequentially from the first through the eighth (four material jhānas and four immaterial jhānas). He then descended from the eighth jhāna in reverse order to the first jhāna and again entered the first, second, third, and fourth material jhānas. "Emerging from the fourth jhāna, he immediately was totally unbound."[6]

Clearly, the Buddha was a supremely realized meditator. He could have elected to do any of a number of sophisticated spiritual practices at the time of his death. The fact that he entered jhāna as his last act speaks strongly to us. Through not only his words but also his actions, the Buddha demonstrated the importance of jhāna at every stage of a meditator's practice—all the way through to full enlightenment.

A number of teachers currently offer concentration meditation retreats and teachings. Not surprisingly, these teachings are not all presented in the same way. Although there may be many approaches, this book focuses on concentration practice as referenced in numerous suttas of the Buddha and detailed more specifically in the *Visuddhimagga* as presented by the Venerable Pa Auk Sayadaw of Pa Auk Monastery, Myanmar (Burma). Our book is designed to be used in conjunction with the Venerable Pa Auk Sayadaw's book *Knowing and Seeing*,[7] which provides very detailed and specific explanations of every step of the practice, the details of which we will not repeat here.

In this book, we share with you pointers from our direct experience—the experience of two contemporary American practitioners who completed the entire samatha path (including the eight jhānas and related practices) under the personal and rigorous guidance of the Venerable Pa Auk Sayadaw during a two-month retreat in Middletown, California, in March and April of 2005. We provide an overview of the samatha practice, from its basic beginnings as mindfulness of breathing to its culmination as a doorway to the *vipassanā* practice. You will find this book relevant if you are interested in samatha as a daily practice for cultivating serenity and insight, if you are called to undertake a more extended period of practice to attempt to access the depths that may be experienced in the material and immaterial jhānas, or if you are interested in the further practices of samatha. We've used the terms *samatha* and *concentration meditation practice* interchangeably.

We believe that one reason modern yogis have found these very rigorous jhānas so challenging a practice is because of confusion about the practical steps that are necessary for attainment. We've also noticed that many people have an underdeveloped conceptual understanding of the jhānas' purpose and that people sometimes misapply the concentrated meditative energy. Our aim is to support your understanding of this practice as the purification of mind and do our best to clarify these issues and misunderstandings. In this spirit, we offer this book—in gratitude to the Buddhist community for all it has given us— as a bridge between modern practitioners and traditional Buddhist teachings.

2

Samatha Practice: The Purification of Mind

WE WOULD LIKE to begin by setting this chapter in the context of the entire path of practice as outlined by the Buddha and preserved in the Theravada tradition. The path to liberation includes three stages:

1. ethical behavior or morality (*sīla*)
2. concentration or serenity (samatha)
3. insight (vipassanā)

Ethical behavior lays the foundation for the other practices. The majority of this book focuses on the samatha practice, of which the possibility of experiencing the jhāna absorptions is a part. In undertaking concentration practice, you will inevitably encounter hindrances and attachments. Although these may seem like obstacles to the practice, working with them actually *is* the practice, when you understand that samatha is designed for purification of mind. How do you know if you are "doing" the practice? Often you know because you are encountering hindrances. This is, in fact, a common beginning stage of engaging the practice of purifying the mind. Purification of mind can be likened to the clearing of a cloudy glass of water. At first, there are particles of dirt floating throughout the water. Over time, with stillness, the particles settle, revealing a clear, sparkling, pure glass of water.

Vipassanā is the third segment of the Buddha's teachings. Through vipassanā practices, it is possible to see beyond what is available to the normal sense perceptions. As meditative capacity deepens, the yogi can see directly into the nature of reality.

PRELIMINARY PRACTICES OF *SĪLA*

Whether you are practicing at home or on a retreat, it is essential to develop the wholesome moral ground from which the possibility of jhāna exploration can most readily commence. The eight precepts and the five precepts, listed below, can be considered as training guidelines that support all aspects of spiritual practice.

Jhānas are a highly specialized meditative undertaking. Daily samatha practice can be a wonderful means for cultivating serenity, developing concentration, and beginning to purify the mind. An in-depth exploration of the practice requires a minimum of ten days to several months on retreat.

The Venerable Pa Auk Sayadaw requires retreatants to adopt the eight precepts, or at a minimum the five precepts. Householders are encouraged to adopt a modified version of the five precepts. The precepts are taken as an act of virtue, a wholesomeness of person, intention, and spirit. Wholesomeness promotes successful *ānāpānasati* meditation and the possibility of jhāna. Inviting wholesomeness and turning away from unwholesome thoughts and actions is absolutely vital to purifying the mind. If you are too distracted by attractions and aversions, concentration practice is not as productive as it could be. There are numerous counterproductive actions that may appear harmless but that do distract the awareness in a way that erodes the practice. Some examples include small amounts of talking, frequently evaluating your practice, and obsessing about food. You need to allow the precepts into your deepest level of intention and aspiration. You must honor the spirit and meaning of the precepts as a way of cultivating the ground for concentration practice.

Eight Precepts (for Use on Retreat)
1. I undertake the precept to refrain from harming living creatures.
2. I undertake the precept to refrain from taking that which is not given.
3. I undertake the precept to refrain from all sexual activity.
4. I undertake the precept to refrain from incorrect speech.
5. I undertake the precept to refrain from consuming intoxicating drinks and drugs.
6. I undertake the precept to refrain from eating during the forbidden time (that is, after twelve o'clock noon).
7. I undertake the precept to refrain from dancing, singing, listening to music, going to see entertainment, wearing garlands, using perfumes, and beautifying the body with cosmetics.
8. I undertake the precept to refrain from lying on a high or luxurious seat or sleeping place.

The Magga-vibhanga Sutta defines refraining from incorrect speech as "abstaining from lying, abstaining from divisive speech, abstaining from abusive speech, abstaining from idle chatter."[1] Idle chatter, both external and internal, must be silenced during a concentration retreat.

Meditators usually take the precepts at the beginning of a retreat. To the extent feasible, honoring and applying as many of the precepts as possible prior to the retreat lays a wholesome groundwork for purification of mind as found in the samatha practice. A wholesome mind seeks and expresses wholesome actions.

The precepts can be modified to fit the life of a householder while living a worldly life, as is common with modern practitioners. Undertaking these precepts on an ongoing basis is a practice in itself, revealing areas of attachment, aversion, and delusion in your daily life. For example, suppose you apply the first precept (to refrain from harming living creatures) to your day-to-day life. Certainly there are obvious dietary questions. Should you be a vegetarian? What if your family pet becomes ill with terminal cancer? Do you put your pet down? When insects invade your home, do you exterminate them? What if your country is invaded by hostile forces? Do you support your country's military in defending itself? These are the types of issues that challenge you to engage the precepts and live them more deeply. Living with consciousness of your deepest intentions cultivates wholesomeness in an ongoing way.

Five Precepts (as Used by Many Modern Buddhists)
1. I undertake the precept to refrain from harming living creatures.
2. I undertake the precept to refrain from taking that which is not given.
3. I undertake the precept to refrain from harming others through sexual activity.
4. I undertake the precept to refrain from incorrect speech.
5. I undertake the precept to refrain from clouding the mind by consuming intoxicating drinks and drugs that lead to carelessness.

The Four Noble Truths

The seminal teaching of the Buddha is the Four Noble Truths:

1. the fact that there is suffering and unsatisfactoriness in life
2. the origin of suffering
3. the cessation of suffering
4. the way to achieve the cessation of suffering

The Noble Truths are the subject of extensive teaching in Buddhism. We refer you to Walpola Rahula's book *What the Buddha Taught*[2] for a more detailed overview of the Four Noble Truths and the Eightfold Path than we will present here.

To summarize, the unsatisfactoriness that is inevitable in life comes from our attachments—grasping or rejecting what is occurring. We suffer when we desire something that we do not obtain or receive the desired object and then either lose it or want more than was received. The origin of suffering is complex. Simply put, it is the belief that the five aggregates—materiality, sensations, perceptions, mental formations, and consciousness—are "me." The average person takes the aggregates as an individual "me"—a separate and distinct self. This imagined identity then seeks to reinforce itself both internally and externally, creating more grasping and attachment. This sense of a "me" also regards the thoughts as coming from an identity. Cessation of suffering, as taught by the Buddha, is becoming free of this delusion that there is an "I." We become free by practicing the Eightfold Path.

THE EIGHTFOLD PATH

1. wise view
2. wise intention
3. wise speech
4. wise action
5. wise livelihood
6. wise effort
7. wise mindfulness
8. wise concentration[3]

As with the Four Noble Truths, entire books have been written about the Eightfold Path. Since teaching the Eightfold Path is not our purpose, we will not detail it here. However, it is important to note that the Buddha repeatedly defines the last element of the Eightfold Path—wise concentration—as jhāna.[4]

SAMATHA PRACTICE OVERVIEW

The word *samatha* can be translated as "tranquility" or "serenity." In the samatha practices, our primary task is to focus on one object to the exclusion of everything else—in other words, to develop concentration. The Buddha taught more than forty meditation objects for samatha practice, which are described in detail in the *Visuddhimagga*. The most widely used of these objects is the natural breath as found in the ānāpānasati meditation practice.

Why would we want to focus on a particular object of awareness to the exclusion of all else? Why would the Buddha have designed these practices? When we attempt to focus awareness on a particular object, one of the first things to happen is that we can't do it. The mind keeps going to other things—thoughts of the past or future, distractions in our environment such as sounds or physical discomfort, and so on. These difficulties, called hindrances, are described later in this chapter. Undertaking this process is useful because the same hindrances that occur when we are meditating also occur in our everyday lives—and ultimately cause us to suffer. This brings us back to the Four Noble Truths—that life inevitably presents us with unsatisfactoriness and that there is a way to meet those inevitable occurrences without mental suffering.

The genius of the samatha portion of the Buddhist path is that it builds our capacity to focus awareness rather than allowing our awareness to be continually distracted and prone to the causes of suffering. Every time we bring our awareness back to our object, we are "building the muscle" of concentration. This can be likened to lifting a twenty-pound weight. When we first lift the weight, perhaps we can't do it very well. Maybe we can't lift it all the way, or we can lift it only a few times before we are overcome with fatigue and need to stop. But each time we lift the weight, we build the muscle. With many repetitions, over time and with consistency, our capacity increases. Eventually, the twenty-pound weight no longer feels heavy because our capacity has increased so much.

In samatha practice, we build our capacity in the same way. Every single time we realize that our awareness has strayed from our object and we bring our awareness back, we are building our capacity to be free from the suffering of life, both large and small. Let's say we are driving in traffic and someone cuts us off. We have a choice: We can allow our awareness to linger over the incident, rehashing the anger or frustration for five minutes. Or, with skillful concentration, we can turn away from that distraction and simply let go. Powerful concentration is an antidote to the hindrances, not only on the meditation cushion but in everyday life. In turn, this concentration and ability to turn away result in a serenity that would not otherwise be possible.

Ultimately, when concentration is honed to a laserlike focus, it enables awareness to penetrate beyond the everyday perception of reality. What do we mean by "laserlike focus"? Settling and stillness accompany deepening concentration. As the mind settles from its habitual chatter, a number of new perceptual capabilities can emerge. When the clutter of compulsive thought is cleared away, the light of awareness becomes powerfully bright. This brightness turned inward in the samatha practice allows access to the immaterial realms that a cluttered mind cannot attain. In vipassanā, when this brightness is turned toward materiality (the physical world) or mentality (thought forms), these can be perceived and experienced in their unconditioned form, without the overlay of conceptual conditioned thought. In this way, concentration can enable us to perceive beyond our everyday, relative reality to the ultimate reality spoken of in mystical traditions throughout the ages. Just as an actual laser beam (which is made of highly coherent light) can penetrate steel, laserlike awareness can penetrate through our conditioned perception of materiality and mentality.

Ānāpānasati Meditation Instructions

In undertaking the ānāpānasati meditation practice, the Venerable Pa Auk Sayadaw references the Mahsatipatthana Sutta, Dīgha Nikāya 22,[5] and gives the following instructions in his book *Knowing and Seeing.* We have paraphrased it as follows:

> Monastics—here in this teaching, a monastic, having gone to the forest or to the foot of a tree or to an empty place, sits down cross-legged and keeps the body erect and establishes mindfulness on the meditative object; only mindfully one breathes in and only mindfully one breathes out.
>
> 1. Breathing in a long breath one knows, "I am breathing in a long breath," or breathing out a long breath one knows, "I am breathing out a long breath."
> 2. Breathing in a short breath one knows, "I am breathing in a short breath," or breathing out a short breath one knows, "I am breathing out a short breath."
> 3. "Experiencing the whole breath body I breathe in," thus one trains oneself, and, "Experiencing the whole breath body I breathe out," thus one trains oneself.
> 4. "Calming the breath body I breathe in," thus one trains oneself, and "Calming the breath body I breathe out," thus one trains oneself. (See Dīgha Nikāya, 22.)

To put this into modern language, we offer the following instructions:

Seat yourself in an upright posture, with your spine straight, your shoulder blades relaxed down your back toward the floor, and your hands comfortably on your legs or in your lap. With eyes closed, allow your attention to be lightly placed where you notice the movement of breath between the nostrils and upper lip—the "ānāpāna spot." The object of meditation is the breath.

You are to know the breath, as it passes the ānāpāna spot, on each inhalation and exhalation.

When the attention wanders from knowing the breath as it moves across the ānāpāna spot, gently return it, without judgment or self-criticism.

One method of concentrating awareness is to count breaths. The Sayadaw suggests counting from one to eight and back down from eight to one, with each progressive inhalation and exhalation as a unit. For example, a single in-breath and a single out-breath is one. Once concentration begins unifying, you can drop the counting if you like.

Another method to develop concentrated awareness is to notice the length of the breath, long or short. This is not a mental evaluation but an aware knowing. It is also not "noting," as in associating a word to the knowing. Simply, upon the in-breath, you know whether it is long or short. Upon the out-breath, you know whether it is long or short. As with counting, this can be dropped once concentration develops.

When you are using the counting, or noticing the short and long breaths, it is important that you don't start to take the numbers or the "short" or "long" as your object, which can easily happen. Your object is always the breath, and these devices are only temporary aids to help focus awareness. You may find these devices very useful, especially the counting, because it becomes very obvious very quickly if you have wandered off your object. However, if they are not useful for you, or if at some time they become superfluous, drop them and simply use the breath by itself.

In terms of posture, you can meditate in whatever position is conducive to practice, as long as your spine is straight and preferably upright. For example, meditating on a zafu, meditation bench, or chair are all fine. Find a position in which you don't need to move around much, if at all, that you can maintain over a long period of time. On retreat, if you are meditating long hours and need to vary your posture more for physical reasons, it is occasionally acceptable to take a lying posture as long as your back and head are elevated, perhaps on pillows. However, this should be only the exception rather than the rule. In our experience, the energy with the spine straight in relationship to the earth and cosmos is much more conducive while sitting than while reclining.

The Ānāpāna Spot

The Venerable Pa Auk Sayadaw instructs meditators to know the breath as it enters and leaves the body at the point at or below the nostrils. You should find the point that is most predominant within this general region and use that as an anchor. The specific spot can be anywhere from the upper lip to the entrance of the nostrils, but not inside the nostrils. The entire sequence of inhalation, pause, exhalation, pause is what is referred to as the "whole breath body." As a meditator, you know the entire breath body only at the ānāpāna spot and should not follow the breath into or away from the body. Sometimes the most noticeable spot moves slightly from one day to another, which is fine. However, it is best for the spot to be consistent for an entire meditation period rather than varying it within one sitting. For many people, as sensitivity increases, their particular ānāpāna spot becomes a consistent, reliable, and even comforting anchor that can then be used to focus awareness on the breath.

With your attention on the breath crossing the ānāpāna spot, it is the breath that is the object here, not the skin. The attention is placed on the awareness of the breath as it goes in and out of the nostrils. In addition, you should not focus on the breath anywhere else in the body, such as the belly or lungs. This is very important! If you do not follow this instruction, your practice will never progress to the point where the nimitta merges with the breath at the ānāpāna spot. (The *nimitta* is a light that appears when concentration deepens and the jhāna factors are gaining strength. Nimitta is discussed in detail in chapter 4.)

As described in chapter 4, this merging is essential for absorption into the first jhāna. Without it, first jhāna absorption will not happen.

The awareness of breath at the ānāpāna spot is not evaluated, judged, or controlled. Breathing naturally is important. Ideally, your attention should never leave this object. During the meditation period, as often as your attention wanders away, it must be brought back to the breath as it passes the specified spot. When your attention wavers or wanders from the object, gently return it without critique or judgment of any kind.

On retreat, even when you are not meditating, your attention should always remain on the breath crossing the ānāpāna spot. With each breath taken, your attention is first and foremost on this object. During every action, whether it be walking, eating, or showering, your attention should be established on the breath crossing the ānāpāna spot. During the night upon slight waking, place your attention on this object. Immediately upon awakening in the morning, place and sustain your attention on the knowing of the breath as it crosses the ānāpāna spot. If your attention wavers at any time, gently return it to the object. Around this time, the mind settles enough to extend meditation periods up to several hours, fostering arising of the nimitta.

Hindrances

Hindrances draw our awareness away from our object. Ultimately, they are the causes of suffering, both while meditating and in our daily lives. The five hindrances are:

1. sense desire
2. ill will / aversion
3. sloth and torpor
4. restlessness and remorse
5. doubt

Sense desire is seeking pleasant experiences through the five senses: touch, taste, smell, sight, and hearing. While meditating, sense desire can take the form of wanting a better meditation, wishing for blissful states to arise, and so on. Rather than being with your object, you begin to suffer because you want something that you don't have.

Ill will / aversion can take many forms, including anger or judgment of yourself, others, or an event. It can also manifest as dislike and fear. In meditation, this can take the form of finding your neighbors or circumstances annoying, judging your own practice, or even fearing that your sense of "me" will be threatened by the fruition of your practice. One of the most common forms of aversion that arises while meditating is aversion to physical pain. As with all of the hindrances, if pain arises while sitting, do not take the pain as the object. This is a difference between this practice and the mindfulness practice as taught in the tradition of the Venerable Mahāsī Sayadaw, in which you would turn your awareness toward the pain if it became predominant. In concentration practice, always stay with the primary object of meditation, which in this case is the breath. You stay with your one object because you are "building the muscle" of concentration, whereas the vipassanā practice is "building the muscle" of being with things as they are, as they arise.

Sloth is often used to describe sluggishness, whereas *torpor* is a drowsy mind-state. In meditating, torpor frequently appears as sleepiness. If you are genuinely sleep-deprived, sometimes it is best to just take a nap. However, if you have had enough sleep, which tends to be the case on retreat, sloth and torpor often reveal an unconscious reluctance to be with the practice and your situation as it is arising. With wisdom, sloth and torpor can sometimes be seen as a sign of some underlying avoidance.

Restlessness is an unsettled mental state, and remorse is the sense of regretting past actions. In sitting, these can appear as restlessness while meditating and as impatience in wanting the sitting to end.

Doubt can show itself as distrust in the teacher, the teachings, or your ability to meditate properly and effectively. With concentration practice in particular, people often have a lot of doubt and uncertainty about their progress as well as their capacity for the practice.

In daily practice and on retreat, nearly every meditator will experience one or more of the hindrances. When any of the hindrances arise, you should determine which hindrance is present. Heartfelt compassion for the hindrance and yourself is a vital first step. The skillful use of effort (discussed more extensively in chapter 4) can also be an antidote to the hindrances in this practice.

On retreat, it helps considerably if you guard the sense doors by keeping your vision mostly downward while fostering compassion and loving-kindness for yourself and others. Also, you can develop a kind of love for the meditative object and the timeless deep silence and stillness that are ever present. This depth of silence and the accompanying accepting contentedness are a balm for the outbreak of hindrances. You can take refuge in the pristine silence of the practice.

The Venerable Pa Auk Sayadaw instructs students that the five jhāna factors are a wholesome medicine for the five hindrances. As we turn away from the hindrances and toward the jhāna factors, the hindrances recede and the jhāna factors increase.

Jhāna Factors

The jhāna factors are by-products of concentration. Usually, we must undertake an intensive period of practice (such as a retreat) for them to arise with sufficient strength to be noticeable. Sometimes people get confused, thinking that the jhāna factors equate to pleasant emotions, as experienced in everyday life. This is a misperception. In actuality, the jhāna factors are specific conditions that arise as a result of the mind unifying through purification and the "building of the muscle" of concentration that develops as we turn away from the hindrances, hour after hour. This is why it can be said that, in a way, the jhāna factors replace the hindrances.

The five jhāna factors are:

1. applied attention (*vitakka*)
2. sustained attention (*vicāra*)
3. joy (*pīti*)
4. bliss (*sukha*)
5. one-pointedness (*ekaggatā*)

VITAKKA

Vitakka (which is translated as "applied attention") is the initial movement of attention to the meditative object. For example, when you find your attention has wandered from the breath crossing the ānāpāna spot, gently direct it back. Each time your attention wanders, nonjudgmentally return it to the object. Initially, your sole "job," if you will, is to apply attention to the object. With many repetitions and a strengthening of concentration, the object eventually becomes more and more stable and you will have less need to continually reapply your attention. Until this happens, though, you must be diligent and consistent (without being heavy-handed) in applying attention to your object.

VICĀRA

Vicāra is translated as "sustained attention." As your attention stays with the object, its coherence develops through the uninterrupted continuity. When your attention does not wander from the object for thirty minutes, vicāra becomes even stronger and is more noticeable.

In daily life, you attempt to focus on the object primarily during formal sitting practice for however long you sit. But you can also return to it lightly throughout the day—while working, at the grocery store, or before falling asleep in bed at night. Whether on retreat or meditating at home, while you are doing concentration practice, your attention should never waver from the object. It is a kind of love affair with the object, which initially is the breath as it crosses the ānāpāna spot.

Although it isn't usually possible in daily practice as a householder, on retreat you should apply your attention to the object and sustain it constantly throughout the day. Vicāra strengthens by maintaining attention on the breath crossing the ānāpāna spot while in meditation posture as well as when walking, eating, showering, and moving around. While doing the ānāpānasati meditation practice, before, during, and after each and every inhalation, pause, exhalation, and pause, your attention is on the breath as it crosses the ānāpāna spot. You never, never, never take your attention off the breath crossing the ānāpāna spot. Every activity is done while simultaneously placing attention on the object. At some point, vicāra can become so strong that the awareness "snaps" onto the object and rarely, if ever, leaves it.

Think of the metaphor of balancing a spoon on the end of your nose. Throughout every activity of the day and night, you are trying to keep the spoon balanced on your nose. Should the spoon slip off, you place it back on your nose and keep your attention exactly on the spot where the spoon touches your skin. When you can apply your attention to the object and sustain it on the object, the jhāna factors arise naturally.

PĪTI

Pīti (which is translated as "joy") is a joy that is without specific situational cause, because it results from the cohering of the mind. We have found the term *joy* in this case to be a little difficult for some students to differentiate from other pleasant or happy feelings they may experience in everyday life. Pīti, as experienced, feels like happiness in the body, although it is actually a mentally induced state. Sometimes it is referred to as "rapture." Because pīti can be so intense in the body, it can actually cause restlessness in some people. This grosser aspect of pīti becomes beneficial as meditators progress through the jhānas because it allows nonattachment to pleasant experiences to gradually emerge.

SUKHA

Sukha means "bliss," but *bliss* is a tricky word because it has so many meanings and implications. Sukha is best understood as a mentally sensed bliss that is also felt subtly in the body. While pīti could be experienced as bodily happiness, sukha can be experienced more like gentle contentment. Sukha is more settled and refined in its feeling than pīti. Pīti is more excitable in its feeling and somewhat more gross. Again, ~~both~~ are produced mentally.

EKAGGATĀ

Ekaggatā is described as "one-pointedness of mind." This mental state is experienced as a focusing of attention and intention, as a collecting and unifying of meditative energy. There is an experience of uninterrupted unification with the meditative object. Think of a flashlight whose beam of light can be adjusted wider or narrower. When the beam of light is narrowed to the visual width of a pencil and the functioning of a laser, this would be analogous to ekaggatā in concentration practice. The attention is highly coherent, increasingly like a laser beam.

In the first jhāna, the above five jhāna factors are present. However, as the meditator progresses to the fourth jhāna, the factor of *upekkhā* (equanimity) arises in addition, to replace the feeling of sukha (bliss). This is because a "feeling" mental state is present in all the jhānas, up through and including the eighth jhāna. In the fourth through the eighth jhānas, when ekaggatā (one-pointedness) becomes predominant, the grosser feeling-tones of pīti and sukha drop and are replaced with the more refined factor of upekkhā. Upekkhā feels like a peacefulness—that all is right and well, independent of circumstances.

As concentration develops, the jhāna factors naturally arise on their own. You cannot stay with the object while simultaneously checking to see whether the jhāna factors are present. Repeatedly checking the jhāna factors splits your attention and weakens concentration, so you will not have enough meditative energy for the jhāna factors to develop. During daily practice, the jhāna factors can sometimes arise weakly, but usually a dedicated retreat is required for them to arise strongly.

The jhāna factors arise as concentration deepens. When the jhāna factors are present, the nimitta (or the light that appears when concentration deepens) becomes closer to arising.

The Venerable Pa Auk Sayadaw emphasizes that the student never takes a jhāna factor as an object of meditation to progress toward absorption / jhāna. The jhāna factors should be regarded as the force that mysteriously opens the student to jhāna, not the object of concentration practice. To progress toward the first jhāna during ānāpānasati meditation, awareness of your breath crossing the ānāpāna spot is always your object of concentration. To focus on any other object is to erode concentration and decrease the likelihood of the first jhāna arising. Concentration wanes every time your attention moves off the object.

Some modern teachings encourage meditators to take jhāna factors as the object. Even in the suttas, with certain translations and the apparent vagueness of the instructions, it can sound as though the suttas refer to taking jhāna factors as an object. Common knowledge of absorptions in the Buddha's day may have minimized the need for him to give detailed instructions on jhānas, as people of his time were likely to be quite familiar with the instructions. However, if you review the *Visuddhimagga,* which presents much more detailed instructions, it clearly states that the meditator should continue with the primary object to maintain the integrity of the concentration all the way into absorption. The Venerable Pa Auk Sayadaw also explicitly instructs us not to turn away from the breath as it crosses the ānāpāna spot at any time during ānāpānasati meditation. Although you may check the jhāna factors to determine which jhāna is present, this should be done only briefly.

In our experience, using the jhāna factors as an object is very, very pleasant but leads only to an intense momentary or access concentration, which are the stages of concentration prior to absorption. (Concentration is described later in this chapter.) This is because as meditators progress through the four jhānas, they need to change the primary object several times in rapid succession and within a short amount of time. Concentration, by definition, is a unification of attention. The most effective way to unify attention is to stay with one object throughout a particular practice.

As mentioned earlier, once the jhāna factors have arisen with sufficient strength, they can be used to counteract the hindrances. The first step is to meet each hindrance with kind compassion rather than judgment. Then you can apply the jhāna factor to the specific hindrance. For example, if restlessness is arising routinely enough to be a distraction, you can begin specifically cultivating bliss. Bliss is the antidote to restlessness. The Buddha discussed starving the hindrances and feeding the factors of awakening in the Ahara Sutta.[6] Each jhāna factor neutralizes a specific hindrance, as follows:

1. Applied attention (vitakka) calms sense desire.
2. Sustained attention (vicāra) pacifies ill will / aversion.
3. Joy (pīti) vanquishes sloth and torpor.
4. Bliss (sukha) eliminates restlessness and remorse.
5. One-pointedness (ekaggatā) overcomes doubt.

Types of Concentration: Momentary, Access, and Absorption

As the samatha practice is fundamentally a concentration meditation, we should take some time to more deeply understand what the word *concentration* means in this context. In English, we already use the word *concentration* in many other senses, which can itself be a bit of a problem. As young people, many of us were told, "Concentrate on your homework," or something

similar, which implies a kind of expending effort or strai
Or, while driving, we may feel that in heavy traffic we must
"concentrate" to avoid getting into an accident. Most of our
modern applications of the word imply a striving energy.

We encourage you to put aside these connotations of the word
concentration in doing this practice. Instead, begin to view concentration as a natural faculty inherent to the mind, which is
drawn out through these incredible practices of Buddhist meditation. We see concentration as a natural by-product of focusing
on one object to the exclusion of everything else. In this context,
then, *concentration* can be defined as the "unification of mind."
You don't need to "do" it to make it happen. All you need to
"do" is apply your attention to your object, over and over, hour
after hour, and concentration will naturally arise. It is like grow-
ing a flower. If you plant the seed, water it, and provide adequate
sunshine, standing over it and exhorting it to grow won't accel-
erate its growth. It will grow all by itself. Once it starts grow-
ing, you can apply skillful means to encourage it (what we have
called "building the muscle" of concentration).

Meditators encounter three types of concentration in the samatha practice:

1. momentary concentration
2. access concentration
3. absorption concentration

It is important to understand each of these types of concentration, how they differ, and how they relate to one another.

MOMENTARY CONCENTRATION

Momentary concentration is the most difficult to understand,
because there are two types. The first develops in vipassanā
practices in which the object changes frequently. In contrast
to samatha practices in which the object is constant, in vipassanā the object is, in a way, changing or "moving." As such, one
could say that the ultimate object of vipassanā meditation is the

present moment and what is being perceived in the present moment (hence, the relationship to "momentary" concentration). Insight-oriented momentary concentration practices are widely used and can be found in meditation such as vipassanā (as it is commonly practiced in North America and Europe) as well as in the Tibetan *dzogchen rigpa* practice and the Zen *shikantaza* practice. The Venerable Pa Auk Sayadaw presents the four elements meditation, which is a momentary concentration practice, as the entry point into the vipassanā practices. We describe this practice in chapter 8.

The second type of momentary concentration arises during samatha practice. The Venerable Pa Auk Sayadaw sometimes refers to this type of momentary concentration as "preparatory" concentration, because it prepares the meditator for and precedes access concentration (the second type of concentration). In samatha practice, the meditation object is consistent rather than changing. Having a consistent object leads to serenity and purification of mind.

ACCESS CONCENTRATION

Meditators can eventually attain access concentration using either type of momentary concentration practice—samatha or vipassanā. However, samatha practices are more likely to lead to access concentration because of their more stable nature. Access concentration is characterized by the significant reduction or complete dropping of the five hindrances and the arising and strengthening of the jhāna factors. For most people, a period of intensive practice is required to reach access concentration. In access concentration, the meditative experience becomes smoother, easier, and more pleasant because of this lessening of hindrances and the arising of the powerful and blissful sensations of the jhāna factors. This allows meditators to meditate longer and progress more easily in the practice. It becomes a positive, self-reinforcing loop.

It is easy to confuse momentary concentration with access

concentration. One difference is that with access concentration, the meditator's continuity with the object is much longer and more stable over time. Another difference is that with access concentration, the object is much more energized and "bright."

Most of the practices outlined in this book are samatha practices specifically designed to settle the mind and develop laser-like awareness, leading eventually to full absorption into the jhānas. Examples of samatha practices designed to develop access and absorption concentration are ānāpānasati meditation (as presented by the Venerable Pa Auk Sayadaw), the *kasiṇas*, thirty-two-body-parts meditation, skeleton meditation, and the *bramavihāras* (sublime abidings).

As access concentration develops, but prior to full absorption, it is also easy to confuse access with absorption concentration. In access concentration, the jhāna factors are present but insufficiently strong for full absorption into jhāna. (The differences between access and absorption are described below.)

Even after a meditator has experienced full jhāna absorption and begins to move through the practice progression, access concentration continues to be used. With progression to each successive jhāna, the meditator first experiences access concentration as the awareness orients to the new experiences and increases in stability.

ABSORPTION CONCENTRATION

The words *jhāna* and *absorption* are synonymous. In absorption concentration, awareness is pulled into the jhāna with a "snap." The beginning meditator cannot "will" the absorption to happen or "make" it happen. Full absorption arises only when the concentration is strong and ripe after many days, weeks, months, or even years of unwavering focus on a specific meditative object. Only later, as a meditator becomes more experienced with full jhāna absorption and more skilled with the progression of jhānas and the five "jhāna masteries," is it possible to enter a jhāna at will. The five jhāna masteries are specific attainments that meditators complete in each jhāna, as demonstrations of mastery, before they can progress to the next jhāna. They are described in chapter 5.

In absorption, in addition to the strong presence of the appropriate jhāna factors, the awareness is extremely secluded and focused, and ongoing concentration is more easily maintained. Awareness fully penetrates and is suffused by the jhāna factors. The *Visuddhimagga* highlights the difference between access and absorption concentration using the analogy of walking. Access concentration is like a toddler learning to walk. The child can take a few steps but repeatedly falls down. In contrast, absorption concentration is like an adult who is able to stand and walk for an entire day without falling down.[7] A modern metaphor would be of a top spinning. In access concentration, the top needs constant attention, wobbles frequently, and falls down. In absorption, the top spins in a centered way on its own.

There may be misconceptions about the experience of full absorption in jhāna. First, there is awareness while in jhāna. It is not a zombie state, trance, or period of unconsciousness. However, there is no sense of "me" while in jhāna. The only awareness while in full absorption is of the object. If meditators have awareness of data from the five senses, it is because they are temporarily out of absorption. The five senses (sight, hearing, touch, taste, and smell) do not arise while in absorption jhāna. In addition, there is no thought or decision making while fully absorbed in jhāna. Beginning meditators who find that they are thinking or noticing input from the sense doors should view this as a slight imperfection of jhāna rather than full jhāna absorption. Meditators can also "pop out" of jhāna unintentionally because concentration wanes and the jhāna factors lessen. It is best not to worry about initial imperfections, which are bound to happen as beginners are developing mastery of the jhānas. As concentration increases, these imperfections wane and stability increases.

Awareness in the jhānas is incredibly pristine, purifying, and indescribable. It is distinctly different from access concentration. Because access concentration can be so pleasant and nonordinary, however, people sometimes mistake access concentration for absorption, when it is not. This is one reason why it is important to receive guidance from a qualified teacher who knows the difference between access concentration and absorption concentration.[8]

Absorption concentration is an incredibly powerful tool for purification, refinement of awareness, and access to realms far beyond normal, everyday comprehension. In addition, this intense focus can be an incredibly powerful tool to apply to the vipassanā practice. Meditation powered by the supercharged energy of the jhānas, or even a strong access concentration, can provide a vehicle to insight beyond normal perception that may not be possible with momentary concentration alone.

We should note that, because awareness is so refined in full absorption, sensory input that would seem minimal in ordinary consciousness can feel extremely jarring when emerging from jhāna. This experience is intensified further when a meditator has completed weeks or months of deep absorption practice and reenters worldly life.

PURIFICATION OF MIND

Increasing the depth of concentration, then, is the method used in the samatha practice to purify the mind more and more fully. Because people know this, we often encounter the question (spoken or implied), "Am I going to get jhāna?" We cannot emphasize enough the potential for striving and suffering that is possible if you obsess about this question.

For better or worse, as this practice has evolved, the possibility of attainments has been one of its main features. And with the possibility of attainments comes the possibility of striving to reach them. It's too late to undo the awareness of attainments with the samatha practice. But what you can do is to meet this aspect of the samatha practice with wisdom and maturity and, if needed, to purify your own striving for attainment (which can be one of the hindrances if it becomes grasping) in the process.

With the vipassanā practice, there are also eight attainments—the eight stages of insight—whether people are aware of them or not. Because these are not frequently discussed, however, people are able to undertake mindfulness practice (as it is done in the tradition of the Venerable Mahāsī Sayadaw) with a productive sense of doing the practice for its own sake. Regardless of whether attainments arise, people find great value in cultivating moment-to-moment mindfulness both on and off the meditation cushion.

So the answer to the question, "Am I going to get jhāna?" is the same as the answer to the question of attainments with vipassanā: there is no way to know what will happen with your practice. Therefore, the most useful and appropriate approach is to undertake the practice as an end in itself. In the case of samatha practice, this purpose is purification of mind. Like the vipassanā mindfulness practice, the samatha concentration practice is well worth doing in and of itself. Purification of mind is its own reward.

A useful metaphor here is of the lottery versus the Olympics. Many meditators come to concentration practice with a lottery mentality. They believe that if they "get jhāna," they have won the lottery, and if they don't, they walk away empty-handed and defeated. This creates a tremendous amount of striving, self-judgment, and suffering.

We encourage yogis to come to the practice with an Olympics mentality. In using this metaphor, we are not emphasizing the competitive aspect of the Olympics but rather the sense of excellence that can be experienced just by participating. In the Olympics, many athletes feel they have already attained something tremendous simply by being in the game. Although most will not win a medal, they all walk away as winners, because they truly participated. This is the case with everyone who undertakes samatha practice. Simply by bringing their awareness back to their object—time after time, day after day, year after year—they have built a capacity that can be applied to many other areas of life.

The cultivation of serenity and concentration in our daily lives is very timely in our busy modern society, in which both are sorely lacking. Through the purification of mind that develops when we encounter the hindrances and are able to let go, we reduce our suffering and ultimately contribute to reducing the collective suffering of the world.

In describing purification of mind, one yogi told us a story about a long concentration retreat that he did. During this retreat, the hindrances arose strongly and did not subside. Eventually, he realized that he had been "holding a burning coal" (a strong hindrance) in his hand for years without even knowing it. Because he was doing concentration practice in which he was focusing on one constant object, he ultimately had to acknowledge and face this long-held hot coal:

> I could see the defilements as the Second Noble Truth—finally see through my own delusion and surrender. I saw the hot coal and really felt how painful it was. After time, I was able to open my hand and let it go. Now I can be with myself and be vulnerable to the truth, both in meditation and in life. I am more able to be with whatever comes.[9]

We have also found some interesting historical perspectives describing purification of mind. Buddhagosa, author of the *Visuddhimagga,* traces the word *jhāna* to two sources. (The Pāli word *jhāna* comes from the Sanskrit word *dhyana*.) One source is the verb *jhayati,* which means "to think" or "to meditate." The other is the verb *jhapeti,* which means "to burn up." Buddhagosa explains that "it burns up opposing states," destroying the mental defilements that prevent the development of serenity and ultimately insight.[10]

Purification of mind can also be likened to a "rock polisher." A rock-polishing device spins like a clothes dryer but contains rocks instead. As the polisher turns, the rocks come in contact with one another again and again, knocking the rough edges and debris off one another. This is similar to purification of mind. Through contact with our defilements, hindrances, and attachments, which are brought to awareness by attempting to stay with one object to the exclusion of everything else, our "rough edges" get worn away. The rock polisher doesn't actually change the inherent content of the rock; it refines it—just as our awareness is refined and purified by the samatha practice, enabling the underlying radiance to shine through.

The samatha practice of purification of mind is an essential part of the Buddhist path. In daily life, it cultivates serenity, which brings a peace and joy to our ongoing experience. It also builds the "muscle of concentration," which can be used to counteract our overstimulated and chronically busy modern world. The brilliant concentration that can be developed during concentration meditation is ultimately intended to be turned toward the vipassanā practice, to penetrate beyond everyday perception and into ultimate materiality and mentality, to the true nature of both the conditioned and the unconditioned.

Given the many important reasons to undertake samatha practice, why has it been mostly neglected in modern times? One reason is the Buddha's statement that only vipassanā practice is required for liberation. Yogis sometimes ask us, "Should I just do vipassanā and skip samatha?" While it is true that the Buddha said that enlightenment is possible while practicing vipassanā exclusively, we cannot deny the fact that the Buddha himself was both a samatha and vipassanā yogi. Not only did he undertake the practice of samatha before his full enlightenment, but he continued to practice samatha and the jhānas on an ongoing basis throughout his life, and even entered jhāna leading up to and including the moment of his death.

Even so, each of us needs to determine for ourselves what is right for our own practice. When practitioners ask us this question, we propose that they look inward for the answer:

- What practice or practices speak to you, call you?
- What keeps your practice engaged and alive?
- What is your "next step" in practice?

Not Good Reasons for Undertaking Concentration Practice

There are several additional reasons why samatha practice has been neglected in modern times. While we could speculate about this, in our own experience and through informal research, we have discovered some unwholesome reasons why people currently or historically have undertaken concentration practice that deserve mentioning.

In undertaking this practice, as with everything in the Buddhist path, your intention is a key component. How wholesome is your desire for the practice? This one factor will color your entire experience. Here are four reasons people might consider undertaking concentration practice that are not very wholesome and ultimately will not lead to liberation:

1. chasing attainments
2. cultivating bliss states
3. developing psychic powers
4. regarding samatha practice as the end of the path

Chasing Attainments

The first unskillful reason to undertake concentration practice is the "notch in the belt" syndrome of gaining an attainment. Undertaking any practice primarily for the sake of logging one more accomplishment is a product of the ego. Ultimately, as with all these unskillful motivations, the motivation itself can thwart the attainment. When a person comes to this practice with unwholesome desire in the form of striving, the practice is most certainly likely to stall out. This is why doing the practice for its own sake—with purification of mind as the goal—is a much more wholesome approach.

Cultivating Bliss States

Some people are attracted to practices that cultivate deep concentration because of the extremely blissful sensations of the jhāna factors in access concentration. This can be both a blessing and a curse. As a blessing, it attracts meditators to nonordinary experiences and allows them to meditate longer and more intently, with little awareness of physical pain or outside distractions. As a curse, it can become a trap, because the practice cannot progress to absorption if meditators have an attachment to focusing on the jhāna factors in order to experience bliss. And as they progress through the jhānas, meditators must be willing to let particular jhāna factors drop in order to move on.

This second unskillful reason for undertaking concentration practice may be exacerbated by recreational drug use. Sometimes people want to replace the drug-trip experience with the jhāna factors, which are seen as a much healthier alternative. While the jhāna factors would indeed be a healthier alternative, ecstatic states are not the purpose of samatha practice. We cannot emphasize enough that the jhānas are a by-product of purification of mind—not the sole purpose. There is a certain self-fulfilling irony that the "reward" of progressing in the practice and turning away from our attachments is the bliss of the jhāna factors. But, ultimately, we must also let go of each successive jhāna factor for the subsequent jhānas to be available. If the jhāna factors become one more attachment, this erodes the purpose of practice.

Developing Psychic Powers

Although not a common aspiration, some people are fascinated by the psychic powers that become potentially available after meditators have fully cultivated mastery of all eight jhānas. In the old days, yogis needed these powers just to stay alive in the woods and jungles with no protection from wild animals. Being able to levitate, be invisible, or merge into a rock were survival skills. But nowadays, the primary reason people would culti-vate these abilities is ego power. Only after they have completed the vipassanā practice, and aspects of the ego have been perma-nently uprooted, should yogis even consider using the jhānas to develop psychic abilities. (For a more detailed description of a modern practitioner who developed these abilities, see *Knee Deep in Grace*, by Amy Schmidt, about Dipa Ma.)[11]

Regarding Samatha Practice as the End of the Path

Last, we have been told that in Myanmar and other Asian coun-tries, people in the preceding several hundred years became so enamored with the jhānas that they wouldn't go on to the lib-erating practice of vipassanā. One of the solutions teachers em-ployed was to instruct meditators to stop doing samatha practice so as not to get attached. Ajahn Chah wrote of "right samadhi" versus "wrong samadhi": "It's like a well-sharpened knife which we don't bother to put to good use."[12] The samatha practice sharpens our awareness to enable us to slice through delusion, but only if we use it in the vipassanā practices of insight.

Despite these "warnings," we believe that the *sangha* (a broader community of practitioners) is mature enough to hold the knowledge of possible attainment as an aspiration while simultaneously staying with purification of mind as what we are doing right now, without striving or attachment. And if we find that unwholesome desire or striving is arising, this is what needs to be purified—not avoided.

Thanissaro Bhikkhu wrote about this paradox in a won-derful article called "Pushing the Limits," which is very appro-priate. "All phenomena, the Buddha once said, are rooted in desire. . . . The only thing not rooted in desire is nirvana, for it's the end of all phenomena. . . . But the path that takes you to nirvana *is* rooted in desire—in skillful desires. The path to liberation pushes the limits of skillful desires to see how far they can go."[13]

Ultimately, purification of mind can deepen from its initial stages in momentary and access concentration to the incredibly potent force of purification available in the full absorption of the material and immaterial jhānas. The "thinning of the sense of me" (unraveling the misinterpretation of the five aggregates as a "self") that is possible in these increasingly subtle states is profound. Ironically, the appropriate balance of effort without striving, and discipline without attachment, is what makes attainment of these progressively higher jhānas possible.

3

Foundational Understandings

THIS CHAPTER provides a context for understanding some of the most important foundations for the initial access to and prolonged availability of the jhānas, and outlines several aspects that support the meditator's approach to samatha meditation. The major topics include:

- putting aside what we know
- silence
- breathing
- resolves
- meditation timing
- "psychic powers"

PUTTING ASIDE WHAT WE KNOW

Many people undertaking concentration practice have prior experience with one or more types of meditation. While learning concentration practice, however, you must disregard each and every other type of meditation you have known, including other jhāna practices.

For example, the retreat we attended with the Venerable Pa Auk Sayadaw included many students who were quite skilled in the vipassanā mindfulness meditation that is taught in the lineage of the Venerable Mahāsī Sayadaw. We witnessed that upon arising from seated meditation, many fellow retreatants began the well-known "mindful walking" meditation. Also, during public question sessions, there were questions regarding how to "be mindful" while doing walking meditation. Often, the teachers responded to the effect that it was good to "be mindful" while walking. Regrettably, the retreat leaders and retreatants were unaware that they were using the word *mindful* differently. In the ānāpānasati meditation as done in this practice, the word *mindful* always means placing and sustaining attention on the breath as it crosses the ānāpāna spot, no matter what you are doing. In other practices, the word *mindful* is used to mean being aware of one's object at all times, even if that object changes. Because of this confusion, in our opinion, some of the retreatants released much of the concentrated meditative energy accumulated during sitting meditation by shifting to another meditation object when they got up and engaged in other activities (that is, the mindfulness of their walking).

Students must also put aside what they know of other methods of concentration practice as taught by modern teachers. Other methods are different, and if you apply those approaches, you may lose the concentration gained and prevent full absorption into the jhānas from arising. For example, switching the meditative object from the breath crossing the ānāpāna spot to a jhāna factor will immediately begin to disperse the accumulated concentration. It will feel pleasant but will gradually erode your ability to move from access concentration into absorption, possibly without your even knowing that this is happening.

On retreat, ānāpānasati meditation is done to the absolute exclusion of everything else. Imagine that you are having a multicourse meal at a fine restaurant. Your task is to consume the meal while searching exclusively for the taste of salt. You do not want to taste anything but salt. In each bite, you want to find salt. Salt, salt, salt—nothing else is tasted. This is the kind of focus to apply at the ānāpāna spot while undertaking any activity during a retreat. For daily practice, you can be more relaxed about varying practices, unless you are engaging in the daily practice specifically to build a high level of concentration in preparation for a retreat.

SILENCE

In daily practice, you should find a location for meditation that is as still and quiet as possible. This could be a private room, an office, or some other location with privacy. While conducive surroundings are optimal, as householders, we must also learn to work with what life presents us. For example, Tina has been known to meditate on subway trains or in bathrooms if that's all the situation allows. You can always be aware of the breath, no matter what your surroundings are. In fact, meditating in less peaceful surroundings can help to build the capacity for concentration. This is why we don't recommend the use of earplugs or eye masks except in extreme circumstances. Using these devices can cultivate a kind of aversion that is difficult to overcome when you return to worldly engagement, especially if you use them for a long period on retreat. In addition, the strength of concentration that can develop when your awareness must turn away from these distractions is in itself helpful.

In terms of silence while on retreat, one of the largest impediments to practice is talking. The busy everyday mind must become still to the point that external and internal talking cease. If you talk even the slightest amount during a concentrated retreat period, your accumulated meditative energy begins to dissipate. While it may seem insignificant to talk a little on retreat, the amount of concentration that burns off when you talk even minimally could be enough to prevent jhāna from arising. In addition, talking activates the thinking mind, disrupting inner silence. We strongly encourage you to make the most of your many hours of sitting by maintaining a pristine container and allowing other practitioners to do the same. Briefly talking to a teacher during interview time or a question-and-answer period are the only exceptions.

Conversely, some practitioners maintain outer silence without silencing inner talk, which can take many forms. For some people, inner talk is a running commentary on life experiences and memories. Others may find constant evaluating and judging of the meditation's development to be a tempting topic for inner talk. All these forms of inner talk must become silent. Another way of framing this is to "renounce thinking" for the period of sitting in daily practice or when on retreat.

Maintaining a vigilant awareness of inner talk is a vital first step. You cannot influence what you do not notice. As such, vigilantly watch your inner chatter with patient persistence. Do this as skillful means, not as a tool with which to judge or condemn yourself. An attitude of loving compassion is the best salve when the inner chatter begins. A blend of turning away from the chatter coupled with compassion for its arising is the best approach. At each developing stage of the ānāpānasati meditation practice, allow your awareness to rest in the silence that is always present. As concentration develops, the silence becomes more and more of a magnet. Later, inner thoughts and outer words drop away, and the silence that precedes thought and expression of words is present.

To begin, direct your attention to the breath as it crosses the ānāpāna spot, on the upper lip just under the nose, to the exclusion of your internal chatter. Do not try to stop the mental chatter; simply do not fuel it by commenting upon it. Commenting on the inner chatter leads to judgments about the chatter and, in turn, to new comments on the judging itself. This naturally compounds the distraction from a passing issue to a time-consuming diversion.

On retreat, as your meditation periods lengthen from forty-five minutes to several hours, the mind settles and the talking becomes subtle, sometimes to the point of stopping. Longer periods of meditation are possible as the jhāna factors of pīti (joy) and sukha (bliss) increase and offset the physical or mental stress or pain that would normally be present. Inner chatter and thinking may diminish to such an extent that they are simply of no interest.

In our retreat experience, the inner mind-chatter did stop. As the silence deepened, any movement of the mind toward thinking became uncomfortable—almost unbearable. In the instances when Stephen experienced the mind turning toward its chatter after deep settling had begun, he was slightly nauseous, almost seasick. The process of thinking after the silence has become dominant feels very coarse energetically. Turning from deep-seated silence to inner or outer talking is not desirable. In fact, we found that when other retreatants tried to talk to us, it was almost painful. We felt conflicted between wanting to engage with others at a personal level and wanting to sustain the pristine concentration. Eventually, we avoided contact despite how others may have perceived this. It is possible to hold an attitude of loving-kindness toward others while maintaining silence.

If held in a pristine state, the dominant orientation of the meditative mind at this stage of silence is toward deeper and deeper silence. It becomes a self-reinforcing process. We found that there is a kind of energy or impulse to act that occurs prior to thinking. As the mind settled, thinking felt uncomfortably coarse. These prethinking impulses were sufficient information to enable us to get up, serve ourselves a meal, use the toilet, and so on. It felt as though the impulse toward food, sleep, and so forth, could be acted upon without directing the impulse to develop into a thought. It was reassuring to find that it is possible to function normally without the usual experience of thinking or internal commentary. Gradually, the "thinning of the me" can become more familiar and comfortable.

BREATHING

The breath is the cornerstone of the ānāpānasati meditation practice. To begin a meditation period with a few deep breaths helps draw your attention to the breath crossing the ānāpāna spot. After a few breaths, do not make any effort to direct the breath. You can also be aware of each breath's duration—whether it is long or short. For Stephen, monitoring whether the breath was long or short was not helpful, but counting was initially useful. For Tina, using the traditional counting of one through eight or noticing (not noting as self-talk but simply noticing) whether the breath was short or long initially deepened concentration. Later, this was no longer necessary and could be dropped. Whatever the duration of the breath, maintain your attention on the breath as it crosses the ānāpāna spot. As you inhale and exhale, your attention should remain fixed on the object. Keep your attention on the object even when there is little or no breath. The attitude is one of being present, waiting for the breath crossing the ānāpāna spot.

One of the most frequent questions we are asked is, "What if I can't feel the breath at the ānāpāna spot?" We must remember that the actual instruction is to know the breath at the ānāpāna spot, not just to feel it. This becomes important later, as the breath becomes more and more subtle. To answer the above question, we first encourage you to have the attitude of being present and attentive to the breath at the ānāpāna spot. Second, know that as your awareness becomes more concentrated, you most likely will be able to perceive subtleties of the breath that are normally beyond your everyday perception. Stay with it and remain attentive. Third, be aware that any place within the region extending from the upper lip and including the nostrils is fine to use as the ānāpāna spot, if one particular place is easier for you than another. Just make sure not to follow the breath inside the body. Over time, if you stay with it, you will be able to use the breath at the ānāpāna spot as an object, just as hundreds of thousands of meditators have done over the millennia.

On a long retreat, especially if the jhānas arise, the breath becomes more and more subtle. There is some discussion as to whether the breath actually stops in the fourth jhāna. We would say that the breath becomes very, very subtle and feels as if it has stopped, although we cannot explain how this is physically possible. The Venerable Pa Auk Sayadaw instructs that the breath in the fourth and succeeding jhānas does indeed stop, citing the Rahogata Sutta.[1] When beginning students check for breath, this checking or investigating mind is outside of jhāna. The investigating mind and full absorption cannot coexist simultaneously. The investigating mind does produce a very, very subtle breath. Due to very strong concentration, beginning students may not realize they are shifting from full jhāna absorption-concentration to the investigating mind, as it may occur in an instant. Because the shift can be so quick, it can appear to beginning students that there is a continuity of breath in fourth and succeeding jhānas.

In either case, the body and mind can sometimes experience a surge of fright at the possibility of insufficient breath to keep the body alive. The experience of bodily fright is fairly normal. It is important, however, not to give in to the sense of panic by taking a large breath at the time of fright or by continuing to investigate this phenomenon. Either action will diminish concentration and set you back in your effort to still the mind enough for deep concentration to lead to nimitta and jhāna. It's best to trust the process as it unfolds.

As the ānāpānasati meditation practice deepens, the pause between breaths may become longer. Maintain your attention strictly on the object. If the awareness of breath is present at the ānāpāna spot, know it. If there is no awareness of breath, continue to focus your attention on waiting for breath at the ānāpāna spot.

RESOLVES

Resolving to stay in jhāna for a specific duration and emerging from jhāna at a determined time are two of the five jhāna masteries. (The five masteries are discussed in detail in chapter 5.) The use of resolves is a meditative skill that you will be expected to develop should your practice progress to the point of jhāna while on retreat. For example, a time resolve such as "May first jhāna arise for three hours" is typical of what we used on the retreat with the Venerable Pa Auk Sayadaw.

We also incorporated the use of other resolves in order to cultivate specific jhāna factors and / or absorption into a particular jhāna. The form Tina used was to very subtly "resolve" for a jhāna factor or a specific jhāna to arise by silently saying a phrase such as "May pīti increase strongly" or "May the first jhāna arise strongly" before a meditation period. Then she would let go of the thought or intention and settle back on the breath crossing the ānāpāna spot. This takes only a few seconds, so as not to dissipate concentration. A resolve is not a mantra or grasping statement. It is not repeated over and over. It is simply a single resolution to open to the arising of a particular aspect of practice.

Stephen used resolves early in the retreat and prior to settling into the ānāpānasati meditation. He would silently say to himself the following resolves, which he composed: "There is no identity in these thoughts; there is no identity in these emotions; there is no identity in these memories; there is no identity in this body; there is no identity in these feelings; there is no identity in these perceptions." He called these "*anatta*, or no-self, resolves." This was helpful to his practice, as it thinned the normal sense of identity to better allow the jhāna to arise. If some other topic arose to be included, he would include it. And he used the regular jhāna factor and jhāna resolves as well. He also found that a silent offering of daily gratitude and appreciation for the ānāpānasati meditation and its progression deepened the intimacy of the meditation.

For us, after the first day or two, the resolves would arise quickly and pass through awareness as an expression of meditative intention. A little later in the retreat, we employed an energetic experience of these resolves without needing to express them internally with words. At the appropriate time, we would open to the energy of these now unspoken resolves. As you move to various jhānas or practices, you can change the resolves appropriately.

MEDITATION TIMING

If you intend to participate in a concentration retreat, we highly recommend that you begin to meditate for longer and longer periods of time prior to the retreat. If you are comfortable meditating for forty minutes once a day, increase to forty minutes two or three times a day. As that becomes comfortable, increase each meditation period to one hour per period. If your preparation period allows, we suggest getting to the point at which you can meditate two hours twice a day. This gives you a very good start. If you are able to begin the ānāpānasati practice a week or two prior to the commencement of the retreat, this also assists your progress.

Once the retreat begins, meditate as long and as often as you can. Ideally, you want to meditate three to four periods a day. If possible, within the first week or ten days, each time period should be increased to one, two, then three hours. "Two hours is better than one hour, and three hours is better than two hours" was the Venerable Pa Auk Sayadaw's direction to us.

Many people think this is impossible to do. This is where it is very important to understand the difference between practices that cultivate momentary concentration and practices that cultivate deep access concentration and eventual jhāna absorption. At the time of the Pa Auk retreat, both of us had previously had extensive experience with other practices that cultivate momentary concentration, such as the vipassanā mindfulness practice, the Tibetan *dzogchen* practice of *rigpa,* and the *shikantaza* meditation practice of Zen. While it was possible for us to meditate for several consecutive hours doing these practices on previous long retreats, we reflected that it was much more of a struggle to do these practices for many hours than it was to do jhāna meditation.

When the Venerable Pa Auk Sayadaw told Tina to do three hours and eventually four hours in the first jhāna, she told him she didn't think she could do it. She had never meditated that long before. But because in the jhānas the hindrances have dropped—completely in some cases—it is possible to feel pleasant and not in pain when meditating for a long time. And when the awareness is absorbed fully into a jhāna, it is quite definitely possible because most outer distractions are not perceived with the senses or are so slight that they don't matter. Even at the Pa Auk retreat, when we tried to sit for hours listening to a talk, we found the experience different from and more difficult than sitting for hours in deep access or absorption concentration. This demonstrates the contrast between strong and weak concentration. The relief from the hindrances, and the blissful feelings of the jhāna factors present with strong concentration, are what make it possible to sit for long hours.

In addition, because Westerners have not been raised for their entire lives to sit on zafus or on the floor as Asians have traditionally been, the Venerable Pa Auk Sayadaw graciously allows people to use a chair when necessary and when doing multihour sitting periods. He does prefer that students use the traditional floor posture, and in fact, on our retreat there were several Asian retreatants who sat only on a grass mat with no cushion! But, for Westerners, the Venerable Pa Auk Sayadaw feels it is most important to do what best facilitates effective practice. So use a chair if necessary, maintaining effective, upright posture with your feet on the floor.

To cultivate both your belief that two or three hours of continuous meditation is possible and your ability to do so, when you do formal meditation, sit for the entire time period you intended before the meditation began. If you told yourself you would meditate for an hour, do not arise until an hour has passed. If two hours, sit for two hours. You need to develop the time-commitment discipline very early on in the retreat. With the bliss of the jhāna factors, this is not only possible but also enjoyable. After two weeks, you should be able to meditate for the entire time period without moving or while moving very little. This may sound difficult to downright impossible, but it isn't. It is a matter of opening yourself to the reality that tens of thousands of meditators throughout history have been able to do this. If you are convinced you can do it, you will be amazed to learn you can.

A yogi asked us a great question in a dharma talk we gave at a long retreat at the Forest Refuge, a retreat center in Barre, Massachusetts. It was something like, "What did each of you do in your own practice that helped you progress?" One of the main things that we both did was to closely monitor both the length of time of our formal sitting meditations and the times between formal sittings. We made sure never to let too much time elapse between sittings, as we could perceive that the concentration would start to wane if the gaps were too long. This meant that anytime there was a meal, instead of adding on a rest period afterward, we might incorporate a sitting after lunch and rest later in the day. On retreat, we encourage yogis never to let more than two waking hours (or preferably one) pass without following it with a sitting period equally long or longer. For example, we might sit first thing upon waking up, then shower and eat, then sit, then take a midmorning movement break, then sit, then eat lunch, then sit, then a movement break, then sit, then tea, and so forth. When we were sitting for two- to three-hour periods, the day would fly by. We would do one sitting before breakfast, eat breakfast, do one sitting, eat lunch, do one sitting, drink tea, do one sitting, sleep. The point is, no matter how long your sitting periods are, try not to burn off your concentration in between or it will never reach the "boiling point," just as taking the lid off a pot of water to check its temperature will delay, if not prevent, it from boiling. Remember even while moving around, your attention is still on your primary object, to cultivate continuity.

"Psychic Powers"

In the following chapters, as we detail our experience of the many traditional Theravada Buddhist practices we learned with the Venerable Pa Auk Sayadaw, some people may be surprised to see these types of practices as part of a traditional Buddhist path, or they may think "psychic powers" are required to complete them. However, using powers beyond normal awareness is a time-honored practice, known throughout Buddhism for more than twenty-five hundred years, starting with the Buddha. We also have precedents of modern teachers such as the Venerable Pa Auk Sayadaw and Dipa Ma, not to mention the many lay and monastic practitioners at Pa Auk Monastery in Myanmar who do these practices daily.

To provide another context, in the Samannaphala Sutta,[2] the Buddha directs that "the mind thus concentrated, purified, and bright, unblemished, free from defects, pliant, malleable, steady, and attained to imperturbability, is directed and inclined to the modes of supranormal powers." It is worth noting that the Buddha does not say *supernatural* but rather *supranormal.* These powers are not outside, or beyond, what is natural. Rather, the meditative powers or abilities used in Buddhist practice are merely beyond what is considered normal.

As the mind is collected, unified, and stabilized through the rise of the jhāna factors and entry into absorption, a purified brightness of mind is apparent. This laserlike concentration is focused and capable of penetrating in a nonordinary manner. It is sometimes referred to as the "divine eye" or "wisdom eye." (See the Ariyapariyesana Sutta.)[3] The wisdom eye is used to some extent in nearly all the meditations presented in this book, including the ānāpānasati meditation, thirty-two-body-parts meditation, skeleton meditation, kasiṇa meditations, sublime abidings meditations, protective meditations, and four elements meditation.

While modern practitioners may see these practices as beyond what is normally possible, we encourage you to remember that thousands of Buddhists have done these practices for more than twenty-five hundred years. The Buddha identified doubt as one of the five hindrances. Your own confidence and strong faith (lack of doubt) will serve you well as you undertake these practices.

4

Skillful Effort from First Sit to First Jhāna

IN THIS CHAPTER, we discuss the territory leading up to full absorption into the first jhāna. For many if not most meditators, this is the most challenging territory of the whole path, which is why we are dedicating a full chapter to it. Many meditators spend an entire retreat, many retreats, or the complete duration of their practice solely within this territory. Applying the foundations discussed in the previous chapters will assist in navigating this important terrain.

ASPECTS OF APPROPRIATE EFFORT

We should note that, while the contents of this chapter are relevant to both daily and retreat practice, much of what is described here is most relevant for the retreatant. Nonetheless, all who undertake this beautiful practice can benefit from a greater understanding and application of the skillful and wise use of appropriate effort, as this is one of the most important aspects of concentration meditation practice.

Intention

Effort begins with intention. Initially, we recommend that you take the time to clarify your intentions for engaging in concentration meditation. Why take on this practice? Pose this question internally and allow the answer to come from a deep knowing within. A wholesome intention is essential. Common wholesome responses include collecting the scattered mind, deepening serenity, purifying the mind stream, and developing a laserlike focus, which later serves to engage the insight portion of the Buddha's path of liberation. With a greater clarity of intention, we now turn toward developing the proper attitude to assist us in this practice.

Blocks to Skillful Effort

Before exploring skillful effort, it is beneficial to understand what actions block skillful effort. There are many ways to slow, if not stop, skillful effort. We have noted several blocks that meditators consistently encounter when undertaking concentration meditation.

The first of these blocks is attempting to use previously learned meditative techniques in this practice. Many people have been maintaining a daily meditation practice for ten, twenty, thirty, even forty years. While prior experience with meditation can be greatly beneficial to people's lives overall, it can be an impediment here. For example, for people with extensive experience in the insight practice as taught in the tradition of the Venerable Mahāsī Sayadaw, being mindful means bringing attention to whatever is most predominant in awareness. This might be the breath, thoughts, emotions, the physical act of walking when moving, or the mechanics of movement while eating. In effect, the meditative object often changes with each new action. In concentration practice, the meditative object remains the same throughout that practice. While engaging in ānāpānasati meditation, the object is always the breath as it moves across the ānāpāna spot.

Moreover, in mindfulness meditation, should you experience pain, you may move your attention to the location of pain as the predominant meditative object. In the past, if you were practicing mindfulness meditation, you may have been able to stay with the pain to the point of seeing its arising and passing, its inherent impermanence. In concentration meditation, should you experience pain, keep your attention on the primary object rather than moving to the pain as the object. Do not turn your attention to any distraction from the primary object; instead, turn away from the distraction purposefully. If you shift from the breath to the pain as the meditative object, the collected concentration begins to dissipate.

Another seemingly innocuous error people can make is comparing their meditation to what they expect to be the progression of the practice. As an example, some people report that after each meditation, they compare that sitting period to their previously identified deep meditations. They sometimes rate the experience. Others report evaluating how strong each jhāna factor is in a particular meditation, comparing the results to previous meditations or retreats. All of this leads to an increase in the comparing and evaluating mind, which also begins to disperse the reserve of concentration that has collected during their practice.

Working with the Hindrances

In chapter 2, we outlined the five hindrances: sense desire, ill will / aversion, sloth and torpor, restlessness and remorse, and doubt. In commencing concentration meditation, you take the breath at the ānāpāna spot as your object. As you settle into your meditation, an initial stillness and silence develop. In this stillness and silence, your submerged (or not-so-submerged) hindrance pattern may begin to emerge. In part due to the silence you are experiencing, the hindrances may be more pronounced than when muffled by normal social distractions such as talking, eating, viewing entertainment, and socializing.

In nearly every type of meditation, you can be plagued by hindrances. However, because concentration practices focus solely on one object, "hitting a hindrance" can sometimes feel more intense than with other practices. One teacher makes the analogy that in momentary concentration practices, because the primary object is the present moment (and whatever is predominant in awareness in the present moment), the practice can feel a bit like traveling down a country lane. If there is a rock, you may hit it, but you may also go around it. Conversely, concentration meditation can sometimes feel like going down a steep hill on ice skates. If you hit a rock, it may feel like a boulder because the effect can be quite jarring and dramatic. Further, since the ground is icy, you may have minimal ability to slow down before hitting the rock, or you may even be surprised by it. You must face the issue of the boulder in the middle of the path (that is, the hindrance arising in meditation), simply because there is nothing else you can do.

With nearly every distraction faced in this practice, the hindrance should be engaged only when it prevents you from staying with the meditative object. For example, if you are routinely experiencing sloth and torpor, disregard this hindrance unless and until you literally cannot find the meditative object. Only when you cannot locate or stay with the object do you turn your awareness directly to the hindrance.

We have found an analogy to be useful in understanding how to work with hindrances in the samatha practice. In past years, Tina was certified as a scuba diver. For those who have not seen scuba divers enter the ocean, they put on their scuba suit, air tank, face mask, and fins and enter the water by walking backward down the beach. The area in the water immediately off the beach where the waves are breaking is referred to as the "surf zone." In the surf zone, the waves are unpredictable. The scuba divers' primary intention is to get through the surf zone and into the calm ocean quickly and safely, without being knocked down by the crashing waves. Some of the time, divers move successfully through the surf zone without an incident (that is, the hindrances do not "knock them off their feet"). At other times, divers are hit by the crashing waves and knocked about. They might be pulled underwater and get water and sand in their masks. Their fins might fall off. At this point, divers must refocus their concentration, stand up in the water, clean the mask, reposition the fins, and resume the trek through the unknown waves in the surf zone. This is very similar to the path that meditators engage when undertaking the samatha practice.

We don't know which hindrances or defilements will arise as small, innocent waves and which may suddenly rear up filled with unexpected power, attempting to knock us off the meditative object. If you are not knocked completely underwater, into the swirl of hindrances and defilements, continue your journey through the meditative surf zone. When the waves are too strong and overpower your best intentions, pick yourself up, straighten what is unsettled, and continue your journey toward the open, calm sea beyond the surf zone. Sometimes it takes many trips through the surf zone. Sometimes you may gulp down a lot of salt water. But, eventually, if you stay focused and persist, you will break through the surf zone and into the open sea. Once you get your bearings, you can proceed to actually begin scuba diving, plunging to greater depths into the stillness where the waves no longer crash. There, it is peaceful, beautiful, and even easy. You can look up to the waves overhead and not be touched by them. This is what happens when the hindrances are quelled by the jhāna factors and you are eventually pulled into full absorption of the first jhāna.

So, when one or more hindrances overshadow the meditative object in the samatha practice, deliberately turn your attention from the meditative object to the hindrance(s) at hand. If sloth and torpor arise, direct your attention specifically and exclusively to the experience of sloth and torpor. Do not analyze or think about the hindrance. Rather, meet the hindrance, drawing it close. Often, if you meet the hindrance directly, its energy begins to dissipate. You may not even "do anything" other than be with the hindrance. During a period of working with strong hindrances, at the start of each meditation period, test to see whether it is possible to stay with your original meditative object. If so, move your attention away from the hindrance and back to the primary object, disregarding the hindrance as you make your way into "deeper seas."

Attitude

When you initially start ānāpānasati meditation, your physical and mental energy need to be high. Cultivating a positive attitude is very useful. If you allow your energy to wane, it will be difficult to sustain your attention at the ānāpāna spot long enough for the jhāna factors to arise.

The most useful attitude is one of openness, acceptance, and appropriate surrender. By openness, we mean bringing curiosity to the meditation—the curiosity of "not knowing" what will happen during each meditation. Each breath of each meditation period is new. This is how you want to meet each breath, as a new discovery. Acceptance means not resisting what is occurring within the experience of each breath of every meditation. As discussed previously, your sole job in this practice is to stay with the meditative object continuously, ceaselessly. We use the term *surrender* to signify letting go of your agenda and willfulness, knowing that the meditation moves, changes, and progresses in its own time. Patiently wait, showing up and practicing—fresh, open, and without expectation.

Persistence

Persistence in this practice means continuing to show up for each sitting period no matter how you are feeling. On retreat, it also means staying with the meditative object as continuously as possible between sitting periods when engaged in all other activities. When walking, eating, showering, and so on, continue to direct your attention to the breath crossing the ānāpāna spot.

Some people experience too much persistence, which comes from trying too hard. This often manifests as restlessness and striving. The opposite of too much persistence, too little persistence, produces laziness, sloth, and torpor. One example the Buddha used to demonstrate the proper tension in our meditation practice is the strings on a lute.[1] When the strings are too tight, the lute sounds strained, and the strings, being under pressure, eventually break. Should the strings be too loose, too lax, the sound is equally poor, sometimes producing no sound at all. When we apply the proper amount of persistence, the strings are neither too loose nor too tight, but have an appropriate tension—and the resonant sound is beautiful. Meditation also deepens naturally when persistence is balanced and consistent.

THE EIGHT LANDMARKS FROM FIRST SIT TO FIRST JHĀNA

The vast majority of meditators who undertake concentration meditation practice spend significant time in the territory preceding first jhāna. We have identified the following eight landmarks between the first sitting period and full absorption in the first material jhāna:

1. first sit
2. nimitta commences
3. nimitta increases
4. nimitta becomes stable
5. nimitta becomes solid and energized
6. nimitta moves toward merging with the ānāpāna spot
7. nimitta and the ānāpāna spot merge and become the "ānāpāna nimitta"
8. ānāpāna nimitta draws the awareness into first jhāna

Landmark 1: First Sit

Most of this book up to this point has described elements of practice relevant to preparing for the first sit. We have described numerous aspects of practice that yogis undertake, both on and off the cushion, in developing concentration.

The span of time between landmarks 1 and 2 can be long. For many meditators, a whole retreat or many retreats can pass without the appearance of the nimitta. Regardless of whether a retreat encompasses the entire samatha path or simply this first landmark, it is vital to know that something worthwhile is happening. Meditators who diligently undertake practice are building the "muscle of concentration," cultivating serenity, and—most important—purifying the mind stream.

Landmark 2: Nimitta Commences

Nimitta is an important component of this practice. It is a sign of powerful concentration. It arises in access concentration as a sign that the mind is unifying. References to the arising of the nimitta can be found in descriptions of modern meditation teachers such as Dipa Ma, who described a light when she meditated, even during vipassanā practice.[2]

The nimitta usually starts as a faint flickering of light. It may also start as a smoky experience of the breath, like exhaling in cold winter temperatures. Others may perceive it as a round light, similar to a train or truck headlight. The nimitta can appear in a variety of colors and shapes. Sometimes the nimitta appears at a distance. Attach no significance to the features or location of the nimitta. Persist with maintaining your awareness on the meditative object exclusively.

The nimitta is light seen in the mind's eye, not light seen with the human eye(s). The nimitta arises on its own as a product of the natural unification of mind that develops with concentration. At first, we cannot will it to arise or make it arise. (Later, as mastery increases, the nimitta arises upon invitation, as do the jhānas.)

Whatever the nimitta looks like, or however it behaves, at this point do not shift awareness to it or look directly at it. The breath crossing the ānāpāna spot continues to be the sole meditation object. As enticing as the nimitta is, don't even glance at it. Despite explicit instruction, nearly everyone tries to look at or move attention toward the nimitta. When this happens, the nimitta usually fades or disappears. It's similar to trying to grab a cloud in your clenched fist. No matter how strong the desire to hold the cloud, it always eludes your grasp.

Many yogis strain so hard to "see" the nimitta that they begin to experience stress, headaches, and even eyestrain. Please do not do this to yourself! The nimitta cannot be either perceived with the physical eyes or produced through your trying or wanting to see it. It is generated in the mind, as a by-product of the unification of the awareness. Additionally, if you want to see the nimitta so badly that the illusion of nimitta arises, this will not ultimately result in jhāna, because it is not actually a sign of concentration. Imagining the nimitta or trying to create it is pointless. As always, doing the practice as it is designed and staying with the breath at the ānāpāna spot as your sole object is the most skillful possible action you can take. So, at this point, keep your attention on the breath crossing the ānāpāna spot despite any excitement or desire to go to, or purposefully develop, the nimitta.

Landmark 3: Nimitta Increases

Once the nimitta begins appearing, it will continue to do so provided that you stay with the meditative object—the breath as it crosses the ānāpāna spot. Further, if you are on retreat, do not allow long periods of time to pass without meditating. On retreat, it helps not to let more than an hour pass without a formal sitting period, thereby increasing your continuity of deep practice. In addition, by staying with the object of meditation while meditating, walking, eating, or lying down, you further develop continuity of practice.

The nimitta will arise more and more often as continuity of practice continues. It will gradually increase in size and be present more continuously throughout sitting meditation and even while the meditator is moving around with eyes open. We each had the experience of seeing the nimitta, on occasion, when our eyes were open while walking or eating. For Tina, at some points the nimitta was visible consistently while walking around with eyes open. This is not required or necessary but can happen. Once the nimitta is present for the duration of nearly every meditation period, it is considered to be stable.

Landmark 4: Nimitta Becomes Stable

The nimitta eventually becomes very stable. Each time you close your eyes, the nimitta is present. It is best to restrict all outflows of attention and energy, keeping your eyes downcast and your movements measured, and staying away from any inner or outer talking. The nimitta develops further if you are patient and vigilantly maintain awareness on the meditative object. If you attempt to go to the nimitta before concentration is developed sufficiently, anticipating its merging with the breath, it customarily breaks apart, fades, or disappears. If this happens, return the attention to the breath crossing the ānāpāna spot and wait for nimitta to again arise and stabilize.

Landmark 5: Nimitta Becomes Solid and Energized

As the nimitta becomes more solid and apparent, it will begin to be energized. Conceptually the difference between the solid and energized nimitta is much like a neon business sign. When turned off, the sign can still be clearly read during daylight hours yet may be unreadable at night. This is due to the lack of inherent energy flowing through the sign. When the nimitta becomes energized, the energy field containing the nimitta becomes crisp and bright. For some people who are not yet seeing the nimitta, at this point in the practice the energy field where the nimitta will eventually appear is palpable.

The energized nimitta is a sign of deepening access concentration. The student here usually experiences the jhāna factors strongly and feels very relaxed yet highly energized. Staying on the object becomes increasingly effortless. Again, there can be a strong desire to chase the nimitta and shift to it as the object, or try to "make" it merge with the breath. Doing so will dissipate the nimitta and weaken the concentration. The process of chasing the nimitta and eventually letting go serves to weaken the hindrance of desire and attachment while cultivating a sense of surrender to the practice as it naturally unfolds, always purifying the mind stream.

Landmark 6: Nimitta Moves toward Merging with the Ānāpāna Spot

When you stay with the breath crossing the ānāpāna spot and do not chase the energized nimitta, the nimitta moves closer to the ānāpāna spot. Without your expending any effort, the nimitta is drawn to the breath at the ānāpāna spot. As they move closer together, stay with the breath crossing the ānāpāna spot and ignore the nimitta, until the nimitta merges by itself with the breath at the ānāpāna spot. When you stay with the breath at the ānāpāna spot and do not chase the nimitta, the two will eventually merge together—in a sudden snap.

This merging of the nimitta with the breath happens only when the time is ripe. It is like trying to pet a very shy animal. If you pursue the animal, it flees. If you wait at a safe distance, however, in its own time, the animal comes to you.

Landmark 7: Nimitta and the Ānāpāna Spot Merge and Become the "Ānāpāna Nimitta"

When ripe, by itself, the breath crossing the ānāpāna spot and the nimitta merge into one. We cannot say how this happens, but it does as the mind further unifies. Once the ānāpāna spot merges with the nimitta, you then have the "nimitta / ānāpāna spot" combination as your object. Throughout the remainder of the book, we refer to this merged "nimitta / ānāpāna spot" as the "ānāpāna nimitta." This is a new phase of practice and a very exciting one! We both had the ānāpāna nimitta break or fade on us several times, as we were initially too excited to wait for it to merge on its own. For some people, during this phase the ānāpāna nimitta envelops the entire body. If this happens, let it do so; just make sure you can still maintain your awareness of it as your meditative object.

Over time, the ānāpāna nimitta stabilizes. Again, surrender your own agenda and allow the ānāpāna nimitta and the jhāna factors to strengthen and deepen in their own time. Just stay with your object, as always. It is common here to feel excitement, sometimes wondering whether this is the first jhāna. Since this is a progression, you can expect to spend a fair amount of time with the ānāpāna nimitta in access concentration as the mind is being purified before the first material jhāna arises. Just remain in silence internally, allowing the practice to do its work.

Landmark 8: Ānāpāna Nimitta Draws the Awareness into First Jhāna

The Venerable Pa Auk Sayadaw encourages yogis to maintain meditative stability on the ānāpāna nimitta continuously for a minimum of thirty minutes (the longer you maintain it, the more stable and focused the concentration is) and then make a resolve to enter first jhāna. If the resolve feels like a distraction and you do not want to use one, you can just wait until concentration is strong enough and then let the jhāna arise on its own. Regardless of whether you make a resolve, only when concentration is strong enough will awareness be drawn into the first material jhāna. It feels like being physically "grabbed by the lapels and pulled face-first" into the absorption. It is very distinct and unmistakable, quite different from access concentration. If you repeatedly resolve to enter first jhāna before the time is ripe, your concentration will wane, being more focused on the resolve than on the meditation object, and you will remain in access concentration. While access concentration is very pleasant and serene, with all the jhāna factors being present, it is not full absorption into jhāna.

SKILLFUL EFFORT

In this practice, there is a vital need to understand the concept of effort and how it should be implemented. Most of us living in this modern, fast-paced world find ourselves rewarded for proactively applying our effort to our assignments. We undertake specific action with a particular goal in sight. We use the skills and tools at our disposal to reach that goal while deflecting interference. Our schools and employers have overwhelmingly supported, rewarded, and even taught this approach. Alas, proactive effort is only half of the spectrum of effort in this practice! There is a very fine distinction between "proactive effort" and "receptive effort."

Proactive effort is more "doing" in tone. It is the energy that reaches out into the universe. Receptive effort is more "allowing" in tone. It is quieter and more inviting. Both energies are necessary in the samatha practice, supporting each other as the practice refines and deepens.

Proactive Effort

Your task in this timeless practice is to identify, cultivate, and maintain intimacy with the object of meditation. In ānāpānasati meditation, this means maintaining your awareness on the breath as it crosses the ānāpāna spot. Period! When the awareness shifts away or falls off the object, gently and nonjudgmentally return it. This is proactive effort. It is the "doing" portion of the practice.

Think of the metaphor of driving a car. When you first put a car in motion, you must employ the "doing" effort of pressing the gas pedal and exerting energy. Once the car picks up speed, you naturally relax the proactive effort and lift your foot off the gas pedal. If you remove your foot from the gas pedal prematurely, the car begins to slow. Now imagine driving down a hill. You don't need to add any proactive effort to the car's speed or rate of acceleration. It can coast all by itself. Adding proactive effort at this point is not only unnecessary; it could be counterproductive or even dangerous.

In meditation practice, you also need to know when to use more proactive effort and when to let up. You need to apply a lot at the beginning just to stay on your object. If you relax the proactive effort before the awareness is stably on the object, the awareness drifts away from the ānāpāna spot. This means that you have let up too soon and that you need to place your awareness and attention on the meditative object once again—and hold it in place—using proactive effort. Conversely, too much proactive effort can turn into striving, which is discussed later in this chapter.

Receptive Effort

While proactive effort is very familiar to most modern people, it is essential to know that concentration practice will not develop to its deepest level of silence and stillness unless you also cultivate receptive effort. We want to clearly state that you never relax the proactive effort entirely, but you do relax it as much as possible while still exerting enough proactive effort to maintain the awareness on the breath crossing the ānāpāna spot.

When you are at a point of practice where you are able to enjoy some continuity with the meditative object, you can cultivate a sense of ease—an allowing sense of receiving, that your awareness is resting on the breath at the ānāpāna spot. This receptive "mind posture" relaxes your personal grip on the meditative outcome. The initial goal of the practice is simply to maintain awareness of the object—that is your only "job" at this point.

Knowing this, you can relax your proactive effort into a receptiveness—a surrender of your desire for control. When you surrender the stance of personal control, you invite a greater, more universal aspect to join in the process. By engaging receptive effort properly, it means you are entering into the flow of the practice—allowing the jhāna factors to arise more strongly and draw the awareness deeper.

Relinquishing your personal will and inviting this bigger, more universal aspect into your practice is similar to using an oar to propel a boat through the water, compared with engaging a small boat motor. You need to engage your own energy in using the oar early in the trip to ensure that you don't run into other objects near the dock. Once your boat is clear of nearby obstacles, you can engage the greater energy of the motor to move more deftly and swiftly through the water. Your receiving effort allows this greater, universal aspect to propel the meditation.

You will know that you are using receptiveness and engaging the universal aspect when you begin to experience ease, coupled with the arising and increasing of the jhāna factors. As the jhāna factors begin to arise—thereby reducing and eventually extinguishing the hindrances—less and less proactive effort is required to maintain attention on the breath at the ānāpāna spot. At first, you need to maintain a good amount of proactive effort. After a while, you can begin to lessen this slightly. As the jhāna factors stabilize, the reduction in proactive effort does not lessen the jhāna factors' intensity, and the focus can shift more to receiving. There begins a delicate balance between lessening the proactive effort and increasing the receptive effort that surrenders to allow the jhāna factors to strengthen in their own time. This shift also reflects a "thinning of the sense of me," which becomes vital in progressing through the jhānas.

Balancing Proactive and Receptive

We cannot stress enough the importance of a vigorous initial effort and a deliberate lessening of effort—an allowing and receiving—once the jhāna factors gain sufficient strength. You could also think of this as "relaxing" into the jhāna. For jhāna to arise, it helps to voluntarily relinquish a sense of control of the process—which, in effect, the practice itself takes over. As the jhāna factors increase, they take over the primary work of maintaining concentration on the meditative object. The sense of personal will and even of "me" diminishes naturally, because it becomes unnecessary. This is very difficult to communicate. On the one hand, we do not want to encourage you to lessen your effort too soon, since doing so dissipates the concentration that is building by uninterruptedly maintaining the attention on the breath at the ānāpāna spot. On the other hand, if your sense of "me" exerting "effort" is not reduced at the right time, the power generated by the jhāna factors does not take over the bulk of the meditative effort, inviting the nimitta to appear and stabilize.

In delicately balancing these energies, the proactive effort gives way to the receptive effort, allowing the more powerful, universal aspect to engage in the practice and energize the awareness on the meditative object. If the proactive effort starts to wane, awareness can drift from the meditative object, which reminds you to "do" a little more and intentionally place the attention on the meditative object. If the receptiveness wanes, a sense of striving can arise, alerting you to relax and let go of your personal agenda. In this way, you balance proactive and receptive effort, and awareness is drawn deeper and deeper into the calm tranquility of concentration.

A yogi who enjoys kayaking told us about *riding the rail*, a term used by kayakers. Riding the rail occurs when kayaking becomes effortless yet very alive and vibrant. Kayakers ride the rail when they are paddling in a waterway and, seemingly miraculously, find the unseen current or movement of the river. The more vigorous effort that a kayaker must expend to keep moving through a still patch of water is no longer necessary. Smaller, more precise strokes are all that are needed to keep the kayak in the very center of the current. In the same way, you can use your awareness of the meditative object to notice when the current of universal energy begins to pull you along. When your awareness is clearly and consistently on the meditative object, you then relax your proactive effort and engage your receptive effort, allowing the current to carry the practice along. You are now on the meditative object and at ease staying there—"riding the rail" of your meditation.

Striving

No discussion of effort would be complete without mentioning striving. In this modern world, we are often encouraged to strive and are rewarded for doing so—for applying "extra effort" to our assigned task. Those of us who are conditioned to be strivers know and likely appreciate the "doing" of proactive effort. Regrettably, an overly striving approach to this practice is fatal. Nothing will capsize a developing ānāpānasati meditation practice quicker than applying too much proactive effort.

For example, when a meditator is trying very intently to see the nimitta, it is easy to try too hard. Whenever there is an end point, it invites the mind to fixate upon that goal. In a desire to reach the end point, the meditator may even believe he or she is experiencing things that aren't happening.

One of the ways we have seen meditators demonstrate striving is in their meditation posture. When striving is strongly present, many meditators begin to lean forward in their chair or on their meditation cushion. (It can look like a horse poised to win a race by a nose!) There can also be a felt sense of really wanting the next goal or landmark in this practice. It is a kind of grasping, clenching feeling in the mind and body. It feels like a contracted muscle straining to complete a challenging task. If you detect yourself falling into striving and overpersistence, start by relaxing your posture and bringing your upper body back into a straight line with the lower portion of your body. You might even find it helpful to lean back from center just slightly. This can invite the body-mind into greater ease and a posture of acceptance.

Incorporating ease into your meditation posture and practice does not necessarily equate to slothfulness or laziness. Those arise when there is too little appropriate tension. If you find yourself slouching forward or leaning backward—indicating too little effort—you should make a subtle adjustment to your posture. For many yogis, adjusting the physical posture also shifts the mental attitude into a supportive and balanced stance.

Establishing the proper balance of proactive and receptive effort can seem counterintuitive. We may believe that the harder we press and strain for the prize embedded within the next landmark, the better we are doing, the more we are accomplishing. The proper approach is to focus exclusively on the meditative object while maintaining a balance of the proactive and receptive effort appropriate to the current situation. Relaxing, inviting openness, and surrendering our ideas and prior experience while remaining alert and focused on our object allows the proper tautness to be present, just as the Buddha reminds us with his analogy of the lute.

Sinking Mind

At this point in the practice, sinking mind, which is another manifestation of unbalanced energy, can be a problem. This happens when your concentration exceeds your physical energy. Because you may be sitting so still for so many hours a day, and the experience of effort has lessened as concentration has increased, this is a delicate time in which balance is helpful. In this regard, walking is another tool that can be used to either increase your energy or settle your state, depending on which is needed. For example, when necessary, it is OK to walk at a faster pace in which the physical energy can be elevated (rather than the very slow style of walking done in the mindfulness practice as taught in the tradition of the Venerable Mahāsī Sayadaw). Or, if you feel agitated, you can walk more slowly to settle your energy. In all cases, make sure that you maintain your focus on the breath at the ānāpāna spot the entire time you are walking.

In this chapter, we have discussed the stage that some people find to be the most challenging and difficult of the entire samatha path—getting through the "surf zone" of the hindrances to the arising of full absorption into the first jhāna. We will next present the four material jhānas, including all kasiṇas used to complete the practice of the four material jhānas.

5

Material Jhānas One through Four and Related Practices

WE WILL NOW EXPLORE the four material jhānas, jhāna mastery, thirty-two-body-parts meditation, skeleton meditation, and each of the kasiṇas used with the four material jhānas. Specifically, we will discuss what we have found to be the best methods for practicing these meditations to the point of mastery.

ABSORPTION — FIRST JHĀNA

Jhāna appears only when the conditions for it are ripe. As a beginning jhāna practitioner, you cannot force the awareness into full absorption or make it happen. You must be vigilant while relaxing into the process—balancing proactive and receptive effort. Either your awareness is pulled into the jhāna spontaneously, or you can use a resolve when you enter a jhāna. Do not become discouraged as you focus on the ānāpāna nimitta, allowing concentration to build, but also do not become overly zealous and use the resolves repeatedly to the point that your concentration wanes from expending too much mental energy on repeating the resolves.

"You," as you usually know yourself, do not enter jhāna. Writing about this experience is therefore awkward, because we may use the word *you* when the experience actually moves consciousness away from perceptions of identifying with the five aggregates and toward what we call the "thinning of the me." In this practice, the veils layered and known as the "normal you" have been temporarily peeling away. A thinner, gauzelike sense of self is what is absorbed into jhāna.

While you are in jhāna, there is an awareness of "being" in jhāna. It is not an unconscious state. You are aware only of the meditation object. In full absorption, there is no awareness of time, the body, or the physical senses. However, due to the depth of concentration, the beginning meditator's mind may be able to quickly shift from absorption to access concentration. Fortunately, it is also possible to quickly shift back into jhāna absorption, knowing this to be a minor imperfection of jhāna. In this case, you may have a slight awareness of time, the body, or physical senses. As the practice matures, this awareness will drop and only awareness of the meditation object will remain.

The absorption continues until the jhāna factors weaken or the time resolve is reached. After jhāna has ended, there remains a deeply felt peace. In our experience, the purified personal sense of consciousness merges into unobstructed, impersonal, universal consciousness. The process of jhāna feels as though an ongoing purification has occurred. Each meditative period in jhāna removes further impurities in the mind stream.

We will not be describing the actual experience of any jhāna for two reasons. First, people using this book as a guide may tend to try to duplicate what we experienced. Second, each meditator's localized consciousness is slightly different. As this localized consciousness enters jhāna and is purified through jhāna, the experience is unique for each person.

STABILITY

Great contentment accompanies meditative stability. At the retreat we attended, the Venerable Pa Auk Sayadaw required us to remain fully absorbed in various jhānas for two, three, or occasionally even four hours before declaring that we had completed this phase and gained mastery. To the thinking mind, a few hours of meditation sounds challenging yet possible. In first jhāna, however, the awareness is so close to normal consciousness that it is quite easy for full absorption to be disrupted. If you are required to stay absorbed in jhāna for three hours as one of the five requirements of jhāna mastery and you pop out of jhāna after two hours and fifty minutes, that period was insufficient for mastery. Also, if while in jhāna you notice the thinking mind making comments, you are out of jhāna. You then begin the two- or three-hour mastery requirement again in your next meditation period. Accordingly, you can expect to do countless meditation periods with first jhāna before this time requirement is satisfied. This allows a confidence and familiar stability with each jhāna to develop.

The Venerable Pa Auk Sayadaw required us to stay in the first jhāna, completing two to three hours per sitting for a minimum of three days—as well as having the jhāna be instantly accessible—before moving on to the second jhāna. This is because each jhāna must be stable before moving on or concentration wanes and is difficult to recover. Subsequent to the first jhāna and for all of the kasiṇas, the Venerable Pa Auk Sayadaw required us to be absorbed in each jhāna for a minimum of one meditation period of three hours.

Should you reach this stage of practice, you will go through the first and all subsequent jhānas each and every time a higher jhāna is sought. For example, if you are approaching third jhāna for the first time, you enter first jhāna for a brief period, enter second jhāna for a brief period, and then open toward third jhāna. In this stage of practice, third jhāna is never directly entered without going through each previous jhāna, in turn.

While there can be some anticipation about the subsequent jhāna, unless you have strong stability in first jhāna, you cannot enter second jhāna. If you try to enter second jhāna too soon, both the first and second jhānas may fade. You would then need to return to the primary object of the breath as it crosses the ānāpāna spot to develop stability with the ānāpāna nimitta before the first jhāna will arise again. The jhānas are a purification of awareness. Each level of purification is needed at each jhāna before you are ready for the next jhāna. As each jhāna is mastered, there is an inclination toward the next higher jhāna. Ironically, the jhāna factors that are unnecessary for the next jhāna begin to feel coarse and burdensome, like carrying too many pieces of luggage on a trip. Most students are likely to feel satisfied releasing the jhāna factors that are no longer needed for the next higher jhāna. If not, then attachment to that jhāna factor is present, and that attachment needs to be purified before moving on.

THE FOUR MATERIAL JHĀNAS AND ASSOCIATED JHĀNA FACTORS

With each progressive jhāna, various jhāna factors drop as the mind purifies and awareness becomes more focused and concentrated. The progression is as follows:

1. first jhāna—vitakka, vicāra, pīti, sukha, and ekaggatā
2. second jhāna—pīti, sukha, and ekaggatā
3. third jhāna—sukha and ekaggatā
4. fourth jhāna—ekaggatā and upekkhā

Five Jhāna Masteries

On our retreat, the Venerable Pa Auk Sayadaw required us to gain the "five masteries" in each jhāna before moving to the next jhāna. The five masteries, which are outlined in the *Visuddhimagga* as indicating that the meditator has demonstrated stability and strength in a particular jhāna,[1] are:

1. to advert (call or direct the attention to) the jhāna factors
2. to enter jhāna whenever desired
3. to resolve to stay in a jhāna for a determined duration and to keep the time resolve
4. to emerge from jhāna at the determined time
5. to review the jhāna factors

Only when the teacher is satisfied that the student has indeed completed the five masteries in connection with full absorption in the first jhāna will the student be directed toward the second jhāna.

To Direct the Attention to the Jhāna Factors

Directing attention to the jhāna factors simply means determining which jhāna factors are present at any given time. In doing this, you can feel whether you are likely to be able to enter a particular jhāna at that time.

To Enter Jhāna Whenever Desired

In order to progress to the next higher jhāna, you must be able to enter the prior jhāna at will. This is one reason why jhāna mastery is so important before moving forward in the practice. If you cannot enter the first jhāna at will, you will have a hard time being able to move to second jhāna, and so on. Only when you can easily enter a particular jhāna is it stable enough for you to proceed to the next.

To Resolve to Stay in a Jhāna for a Determined Duration and to Keep the Time Resolve

As we have discussed, on our retreat the Sayadaw required that we progressively increase our time resolves to the point where we could stay in a jhāna for either two or three hours without "popping out" prematurely. This applied for every jhāna using ānāpānasati as the object, as well as every kasiṇa in every jhāna. As with other resolves, when you have attained some stability with a particular jhāna, you then resolve before entering the jhāna to stay in for the specified amount of time. The resolve might be, "May I remain in the first jhāna for three hours." You then enter the jhāna. Upon exiting the jhāna (after checking the jhāna factors, as described below), you look at a clock to see whether you met the time resolve. If you did not, then you attempt it again at a later sitting.

To Emerge from Jhāna at the Determined Time

If you have met the time resolve, as described above, you will emerge at the determined time. This is also important because you don't want to stay in a jhāna longer than necessary as you progress in the practice. For example, if you are moving to fourth jhāna, you may need to spend only five minutes each in first, second, and third jhāna on your way up the progression. If you cannot reliably enter and exit jhānas in a timely manner, you will spend too long in the prior jhānas and may not meet your time resolve for the next jhāna as required.

To Review the Jhāna Factors (Check the Bhavanga)

Reviewing the jhāna factors is important because you want to understand which jhāna you were actually experiencing, to ensure integrity of the progression. This can be done by checking the bhavanga to see which jhāna factors were present in the prior mind-moment.

Of all the topics covered here, the bhavanga is the one we least understand conceptually. Given that we are not Buddhist scholars, we will focus on explaining how bhavanga is actually used in jhāna practice.

The bhavanga is located in the heart region. The Venerable Pa Auk Sayadaw instructs that, according to the Suttanta method, it is also metaphorically called the "mind-door" because mind-door cognitive processes such as jhāna cognitive processes, including the jhāna factors, arise depending on it. When you check the jhāna factors, you must first discern that bhavanga mind-door. When jhāna objects, such as the ānāpāna nimitta, appear in that mind-door, you can see jhāna factors in it because jhāna factors arise depending on the mind-door.

You examine the bhavanga with the wisdom eye after exiting jhāna and before entering the next higher jhāna to determine which jhāna factors are, or were, present. It is impossible to examine the jhāna factors or bhavanga while in jhāna because in jhāna there is no volition or thinking. When you are checking the jhāna factors, you are in access concentration, not absorption.

Somehow, following the time when the student is first able to enter jhāna, the ability to discern the jhāna factors in the bhavanga seems to emerge naturally. We had no idea how this would occur when we first heard about it at the retreat. We thought it might be impossible to see into the bhavanga with the wisdom eye. Yet with the wisdom eye functioning, the jhāna factors can be seen in the bhavanga.

Once your awareness is stable within a jhāna, the instruction is to look very briefly with the wisdom eye (after exiting the jhāna) to determine whether you can see into the bhavanga. After the next sitting, at its end, check briefly whether you can see each of the five jhāna factors (vitakka, vicāra, pīti, sukha, and ekaggatā) in the bhavanga. Only at this time do you attempt the remaining four masteries. At the end of that sitting, again check the bhavanga to see whether the five jhāna factors were present.

At a later sitting, you can attempt all five masteries and then check all five jhāna factors at once, as a unified whole.

In all these cases, you are not looking with the normal eye(s) toward the heart area to see the bhavanga. The wisdom eye develops through the process of purification of mind and becomes quite powerful as a result of the bright energy of intense concentration. Reviewing the jhāna factors in the bhavanga is required to master each of the subsequent jhānas as well.

SECOND JHĀNA

Following attainment of the five jhāna masteries in the first jhāna, the teacher instructs the student to proceed to second jhāna. Having attained the five masteries of first jhāna, we found that we were instinctively oriented toward second jhāna. The second jhāna has pīti, sukha, and ekaggatā as its jhāna factors. It does not have vitakka or vicāra, as they have dropped away.

Return to the ānāpāna nimitta in meditation. If the nimitta is not present, continue focusing on the breath crossing the ānāpāna spot until ānāpāna nimitta again arises. Usually, if you have entered first jhāna, the ānāpāna nimitta is readily available, presuming outer and inner talk remain silent and the attention on the object is ongoing. Shortly after you start with your attention on the breath crossing the ānāpāna spot, the ānāpāna nimitta appears strong and clearly present. Then, cultivate the first five jhāna factors (vitakka, vicāra, pīti, sukha, and ekaggatā) and enter first jhāna. Always enter first jhāna before proceeding to second jhāna. In this stage of practice, at no time do you jump over any jhāna (meaning you do not start with third jhāna without having proceeded through first jhāna and second jhāna). On the first attempt, do first jhāna for an extended period until it is stable and then make a resolve for second jhāna. Later, you can spend only a few minutes in first jhāna and then go on to second jhāna.

When you enter second jhāna, two of the jhāna factors of first jhāna (vitakka and vicāra) drop away. The jhāna factors that are unnecessary for successively higher jhānas drop upon entering the higher jhāna. Again, when you are ready, a resolve is made, and, if concentration is strong and the time is ripe, awareness is drawn into second jhāna.

Interestingly, each jhāna has a feel, a flavor, or an intuitive taste that is different from the other jhānas. With time and practice, you may learn to experientially distinguish which jhāna is present. You should quickly review the bhavanga after exiting jhāna to determine which jhāna factors were present in that jhāna. This confirms which jhāna was entered.

Again, at our retreat, the Venerable Pa Auk Sayadaw required jhāna mastery of the second jhāna. This means spending three continuous hours in the second jhāna during one period of meditation. In other words, the mastery requirement cannot be satisfied by, say, being in second jhāna for one hour during one meditation period and for two hours during another meditation period and adding them together. Jhāna stability, meaning fulfilling the five jhāna masteries, is required to fully experience each jhāna and to have the purification and jhāna energy to proceed with stability to the next higher jhāna. Once the five jhāna masteries are achieved in the second jhāna, you are directed to the third jhāna.

Third Jhāna

The third jhāna has only sukha and ekaggatā as its jhāna factors. Continue focusing on the ānāpāna nimitta. If the ānāpāna nimitta is not available, focus on the breath crossing the ānāpāna spot until the nimitta appears and merges with the spot. Proceed to once again enter and exit the first and second jhānas as before. The time spent in the first and second jhānas is brief. As soon as you feel the stability and bright, clear energy of the first jhāna, exit first jhāna. Upon full absorption into second jhāna, vitakka and vicāra drop, as they are unnecessary for second jhāna.

Pīti is a mental state that produces a corresponding bodily sensation of happiness, almost an excitement. As before, when opening to third jhāna, the jhāna factors of second jhāna feel unnecessary, almost a burden. Sukha as a deep feeling of bliss is very appropriate when developing the third-jhāna factors. Ekaggatā is unified, focused awareness. The meditative attention and awareness unify. No extra effort is exerted. Awareness is drawn into third jhāna with the jhāna factors of sukha and ekaggatā. The third jhāna feels more refined and pure than the second jhāna.

Each successively higher jhāna is easier to maintain, as it is further from ordinary consciousness, so the senses are less easily distracted. We found each jhāna to be independently wonderful. Although each jhāna was very satisfying, once the five jhāna masteries were achieved, there was an obvious movement, almost an attraction, toward the next higher jhāna.

FOURTH JHĀNA

Once the five jhāna masteries have been reached with the third jhāna, proceed to fourth jhāna. Begin by discarding and turning away from sukha, as it is no longer necessary for the fourth jhāna. Sukha is replaced from the fourth jhāna through the four immaterial jhānas by upekkhā (equanimity). Or, as concentration focuses into one-pointedness and equanimity, sukha can begin to wane on its own. Fourth jhāna has ekaggatā (one-pointedness) and upekkhā (equanimity) as its jhāna factors. Upekkhā replaces sukha as a more refined and less gross mentally produced feeling-state, which will be present throughout the rest of the jhānas. Focus on the ānāpāna nimitta and enter first jhāna with its five jhāna factors (vitakka, vicāra, pīti, sukha, and ekaggatā). After a few minutes in the stability of first jhāna, exit first jhāna and enter second jhāna, with the factors of second jhāna (pīti, sukha, and ekaggatā). When stability in the second jhāna is reached for a few minutes, exit second jhāna and use the nimitta to enter third jhāna. The third-jhāna factors (sukha and ekaggatā) are present prior to entering third jhāna. The first time fourth jhāna is attempted, you may stay in third jhāna for an extended period to ensure stability. Over time, a brief stay is all that is needed to confirm the stability and energy of the third jhāna, as with the prior two jhānas. Exit third jhāna and feel the inclination toward ekaggatā and upekkhā.

Ekaggatā and upekkhā feel very full, grounded, and satisfying without having a quality of excitement as in the second and third jhānas. Stephen recalls anticipating that he would find the dropping of sukha to be difficult because of its pleasurable quality. When moving toward fourth jhāna, though, sukha feels unnecessary. The one-pointedness (ekaggatā) and equanimity (upekkhā) are very complete. It is very difficult to be distracted when meditating with ekaggatā and upekkhā.

When these two jhāna factors are strong and the nimitta is powerful, awareness is drawn into fourth jhāna. The shift from third jhāna to fourth jhāna is significant. Moving from first jhāna to second jhāna or from second jhāna to third jhāna represents a slight change in jhāna factors. Experientially, these first three material jhānas feel more similar to one another. You must be willing to set aside all the joyous and blissful bodily sensations produced by the mental states of pīti and sukha in the first three jhānas to focus on ekaggatā and upekkhā in the fourth jhāna. While some people may presume that the fourth jhāna is more challenging because the bliss is much more subtle and impersonal, it is available by trusting the teachings and not just seeking pleasurable experiences. Being willing to develop ekaggatā and upekkhā to the exclusion of the other jhāna factors is natural after mastering third jhāna.

By the time a meditator is close to entering fourth jhāna, the normal breath has become very, very shallow and subtle.

The *Visuddhimagga* states that the breath stops in the fourth jhāna.[2] Experientially, it feels as though it has stopped. What is important is not to be concerned about this issue. Any attention to whether there is, in fact, breath diverts the meditative concentration, making fourth jhāna unavailable. Specifically, there can be a bodily felt sense of fright when meditating with the nimitta as fourth jhāna ripens. This is because the body senses there is insufficient oxygen to live. Resist the urge to take a deep breath to pacify this fright. A deep breath at this time disrupts the development of ekaggatā and upekkhā, and fourth jhāna drifts further away. The fear of having insufficient breath does, in fact, pass. Allow it to do so.

Check the jhāna factors in access concentration and make the resolve for fourth jhāna. Alternatively, when ripe, the deep concentration draws the awareness into fourth jhāna. Proceed as before to obtain five jhāna masteries for fourth jhāna.

FURTHER PRACTICES WITH THE MATERIAL JHĀNAS

Once the first four jhānas are stable, you and the teacher may agree that you should go on to additional samatha practices. In this case, you will do the following meditative practices in the following order:

1. thirty-two-body-parts meditation
2. skeleton meditation
3. white kasiṇa (All the kasiṇa meditations are initially completed upon attaining the first through fourth jhānas using each progressive kasiṇa as the object.)
4. nila (brown / black / blue) kasiṇa
5. yellow kasiṇa
6. red kasiṇa
7. earth kasiṇa

8. water kasiṇa
9. fire kasiṇa
10. wind kasiṇa
11. light kasiṇa
12. space kasiṇa

We will now review the thirty-two-body-parts meditation, skeleton meditation, and all kasiṇa meditations through the fourth jhāna, in turn.

Thirty-two-Body-Parts Meditation

Once you have attained jhāna mastery of the fourth jhāna using ānāpānasati meditation, the teacher will direct you to practice thirty-two-body-parts meditation. This meditation is undertaken to further loosen your identification with the body, which allows for less attachment to materiality and self-identity as jhāna practice develops toward the immaterial jhānas. It also lays the foundation for nonattachment to the body in order to see the *rūpa-kalāpas* later in the vipassanā practice. (Rūpa-kalāpas are the subatomic particles that are the basis of all materiality. They are described in chapter 8, which presents the four elements meditation.)

Here is a quick review: First, enter and pass through the first, second, third, and fourth jhānas using the ānāpāna nimitta as the object. Experience each of the four material jhānas with their corresponding jhāna factors. Complete the five jhāna masteries for each jhāna. Quickly check the bhavanga after exiting each jhāna to ensure that the corresponding jhāna factors were present in that particular jhāna. Exit each jhāna only when the stability and jhāna energy are strongly experienced. Once out of the fourth jhāna, direct the strong, clear, bright energy of unified awareness—the wisdom eye—to the body as described below. The body parts are listed in groups because, at a later point, you will discern them together in these groups.

Earth Element Parts
- body parts 1–5: head hairs, body hairs, nails, teeth, and skin
- body parts 6–10: flesh, sinews, bones, bone marrow, and kidneys
- body parts 11–15: heart, liver, membranes, spleen, and lungs
- body parts 16–20: intestines, mesentery (this connects the small intestine to the abdominal wall), undigested food, feces, and brain

Water Element Parts
- body parts 1–6: bile, phlegm, pus, blood, sweat, and fat
- body parts 7–12: tears, grease, saliva, snot, synovial fluid (this lubricates joints), and urine

Initially, locate each part (such as head hairs) with the wisdom eye and observe it internally. Carefully examine and deeply know each part so that you can know it in the body in one instant. Should the brightness of concentrated awareness fade during this practice, go back to the jhānas using the ānāpāna nimitta as the object, progressing through the first, second, third, and fourth jhānas for a meditation period to reestablish strong concentration. Then resume the thirty-two-body-parts meditation.

See each body part very clearly. You should know characteristics such as the location, color, and contour before passing on to the next body part. For example, discern the blood everywhere in the body at once with your eyes closed. Experientially know the flow, pressure, and color of blood within the body. Actually see these with the wisdom eye. Once you can easily locate each earth element body-part in your own body, attempt to see all the body parts one through five together as a unit. You will eventually do this for each group of body parts in the earth element and water element.

When you can "see" with the jhāna-energized wisdom eye

all the elements of earth and water discretely and as subgroups, look at the earth element group, then the water element group, as a whole. When you have learned to do this quickly and thoroughly, see the earth element and water element groups together, viewing each element separately and as a unit of either earth or water, as well as the whole of thirty-two-body-parts meditation. Although this sounds challenging, with the powerful concentration functioning as the wisdom eye, it is possible.

After you see all distinct body parts exhaustively with the wisdom eye and can experience them distinctly and together at once, try to see each distinct body part in someone else, usually someone nearby in the meditation hall. Try to see each distinct part in the other using the wisdom eye, sometimes with the eyes open and other times with the eyes closed. Once you have done this successfully, continue with every person, animal, or other being in the world. Again, if you begin to lose energy while completing the thirty-two-body-parts meditation, go through the full four material jhānas using the ānāpāna nimitta as the object and then return to the thirty-two-body-parts meditation.

Eventually, you become able to discern every being (human, animal, or other) in all directions as the thirty-two body parts, earth element, and water element, and combined as one of thirty-two-body-parts meditation. When this has been completed, you will move on to skeleton meditation.

This may sound as if it would take weeks or months to complete, but due to the strong concentration produced by the jhānas, it took us about two days to complete. While the time it takes may vary from student to student, the point is that it is sometimes possible to move quickly due to the laserlike clarity powered by the jhānas.

Skeleton Meditation

Pass through the first, second, third, and fourth jhānas using the ānāpāna nimitta as the object, in preparation for skeleton meditation. This is done to maintain the brilliant concentration.

Next, direct the wisdom eye to the bones of your own skeleton. Since you previously saw your own skeleton in the course of the thirty-two-body-parts meditation, returning to this practice is fairly effortless. The skeleton is seen as a whole. Look for color variations, breaks, and cracks in the bones. Hold this sight with the wisdom eye during meditation. After seeing the skeleton in its entirety in one instant, develop a feeling of repulsion toward the skeleton.

Repulsiveness (*patikula* or *asubha*) is used in various meditations to loosen the identification with materiality and self-identity. We develop this repulsion toward our own body because this loosening of the identification with the body facilitates successfully entering the kasiṇas and upper immaterial jhānas. Look with the wisdom eye for the frailties of the skeleton.

As repulsion toward the skeleton strengthens, the mental image of the skeleton eventually ceases and the skeleton as a physical identity drops away. The sense of the repulsiveness of the skeleton then remains as the meditative object.

As the strength of this repulsive meditation develops, first jhāna can arise using the repulsiveness of the skeleton as the meditative object. Look exhaustively to see the "skeleton as repulsive" in your own body. When you are successful, see the "skeleton as repulsive" in another person, with your eyes closed. Repeat this with others until you can quickly move your attention from person to person and see only the repulsiveness of the skeleton. Once you have satisfactorily accomplished this, see the "skeleton as repulsive" in every body in all directions throughout the world. Seeing the skeleton clearly in this meditation is helpful, as this can be the entry point into white kasiṇa later. Also, this meditation helps to further relax your identification with the physical body. In the immaterial jhānas, the yogi's personal localized consciousness must be free to absorb into the more impersonal consciousnesses of each upper jhāna. Once you have completed skeleton meditation, you are ready for white kasiṇa practice.

Kasiṇas

Kasiṇas are disclike images of various colors or elements used as objects of meditation. The meditator enters the jhānas using the different kasiṇas, each of which has a distinct flavor of experience. Progressing through the kasiṇas in the following order allows a further thinning and purifying of the meditator's consciousness. The kasiṇas are undertaken in this specific order because each progressive kasiṇa is more refined and insubstantial as a meditative object. This prepares the meditator for the subtle objects of meditation in the upper immaterial jhānas. Also, with each subsequent kasiṇa, the meditator's awareness becomes more purified, more refined, and less dense. This is preparing the awareness to enter the immaterial jhānas.

Finding the proper color for the color kasiṇas can be tricky. You can use the various colors in the body as witnessed in the thirty-two-body-parts meditation. Using the meditator's own body parts is the traditional instruction. In ancient times, this undoubtedly made the practice easier because the color was always available to the meditator. However, if you prefer, you can also use the colors of nature, such as flowers, soil, trees, and clouds. In either case, you have located the optimal color when you close your eyes and can see the color clearly and distinctly in your mind's eye. Alternately, if using an object in nature, first observe the color with eyes open. When you can see the color very clearly with eyes shut, you can commence the kasiṇa meditation for that specific color.

MEDITATIVE PROCEDURE FOR EACH KASIṆA IN THE MATERIAL JHĀNAS (ONE THROUGH FOUR)

The process is the same for each kasiṇa through the first, second, third, and fourth jhānas. Before you try to take an external object for a kasiṇa, such as earth kasiṇa, enter the first, second, third, and fourth jhānas, preferably using the ānāpāna nimitta or white kasiṇa as the object. Emerging from the fourth jhāna, the mind is very concentrated and powerful, thus making the task of taking a kasiṇa as an object, such as earth kasiṇa, much easier. Once you are proficient with a kasiṇa, you need only pay attention to a previous kasiṇa image for the nimitta to arise.

Locate the proper color for the kasiṇa you are undertaking. You can use the color or other characteristic (earth, water, fire, and so on) of the specific kasiṇa as the meditative object when you can see it with eyes closed. When the jhāna factors are strengthening, the kasiṇa becomes energized and clearly visible. You can sense when the kasiṇa becomes stable, as you did with the ānāpāna nimitta previously. The kasiṇa is available whenever you close your eyes, even if only for a moment. Once the image of the kasiṇa is stable and energized, begin to expand the kasiṇa. The kasiṇa may expand on its own. If not, use a subtle intention to expand the kasiṇa.

Expand the kasiṇa a few inches at a time. Should the kasiṇa become thin or should you see apparent holes in the kasiṇa with the wisdom eye, the kasiṇa has been expanded too quickly. Use a subtle intention to retract the kasiṇa to a smaller size that feels more stable and cohesive. Meditate upon the kasiṇa as an object until it is stable and the jhāna factors are energized. The jhāna factors increase as the meditation deepens. As the jhāna factors become stronger, the kasiṇa can eventually be expanded to encompass the entire world, including you. Up to this point, while focusing on the kasiṇa, the concentration is at the level of access concentration.

When the endless kasiṇa image is independently stable and bright, focus on a small spot on the expanded kasiṇa. This spot becomes the new object of meditation. This is like looking into the open, expansive sky and being fixated upon a specific, particular spot. When meditative concentration is strong and all the jhāna factors needed for that jhāna are strong, the spot on the kasiṇa draws awareness into first jhāna. Complete all five jhāna masteries for the first jhāna using a particular kasiṇa as an object. Then progress to the next successively higher material jhāna to complete all four material jhānas and the five masteries in each, using that kasiṇa as an object.

We will refer back to this process with each kasiṇa rather than laboriously restating it for each jhāna of each kasiṇa. Again, the sequence for initially cultivating the kasiṇas is as follows:

1. white kasiṇa
2. nila kasiṇa
3. yellow kasiṇa
4. red kasiṇa
5. earth kasiṇa
6. water kasiṇa
7. fire kasiṇa
8. wind kasiṇa
9. light kasiṇa
10. space kasiṇa

WHITE KASIṆA

To start white kasiṇa practice, go through the first, second, third, and fourth jhānas using the ānāpāna nimitta as the object. Then quickly undertake and complete the thirty-two-body-parts meditation. See the skeleton separately from the other parts of the thirty-two-body-parts meditation and take it as the meditative object. Use the wisdom eye to locate the whitest part of the skeleton; often the back of the skull is used as a meditative object given its color, size, and round shape (resembling a disc). Take the whiteness of the back of the skull, or a different part of the skeleton, as the meditative object.

See the white color, taken from the back of the skull where the nimitta previously appeared, with your eyes closed. If you cannot find the proper white to be taken as an object from your own body, use the white from an object in nature—a cloud or other source, such as a flower. It needs to be a white that intuitively feels like the right color. From the strength of the fourth jhāna, the factors for first jhāna (vitakka, vicāra, pīti, sukha, and ekaggatā) begin to arise. At this time, the white held as the object begins to take the form of a disc. A white disc is then the natural object of meditation. This white object becomes a stable meditative object. The stability of the kasiṇa becomes apparent through the independently energized, bright white kasiṇa. Expand the kasiṇa to encompass the entire world. This may happen with no effort on your part. If the kasiṇa does not automatically expand, expand it in each meditation period using subtle intention.

At this point, there is white in every direction, as far as the wisdom eye can see. The vast whiteness includes you. When the expanded white is everywhere and that object is stable, choose a specific point in the white upon which to place your attention. Over time, your meditative attention effortlessly locks onto a specific, small spot on the expanded kasiṇa. Although this may sound strange to the thinking mind, this is quite comfortable to do. The meditative attention falls naturally on a specific spot on the expanded white kasiṇa, and that becomes the new meditative object.

Eventually, as the jhāna factors increase, this spot on the expanded white kasiṇa draws awareness into jhāna. Alternatively, you can make a resolve for jhāna. Using the same process as before, progress through the first, second, third, and fourth jhānas using white kasiṇa as an object, discerning the jhāna factors after each meditation period in jhāna and staying with the particular jhāna until the five masteries for each jhāna have been achieved.

Again, if you try to move to the next jhāna or kasiṇa without fully gaining all the five jhāna masteries in each of the four material jhānas using that particular kasiṇa, it is difficult if not impossible to take the next kasiṇa in the sequence as an object and have it be stable enough for jhāna.

Patient, persistent practice with each jhāna is needed to continue working through the kasiṇas. After white kasiṇa is used to enter the four jhānas, the white kasiṇa now becomes the beginning meditative object for the remaining kasiṇas. This means that at the start of each meditation period, you intentionally see the white kasiṇa. Once the white kasiṇa is stable and energized, expand it until the jhāna factors for first jhāna are strong. Allow your awareness to be drawn to a spot on the expanded white color. The spot chosen on the fully expanded white color draws awareness into first jhāna. Pass through each of the first four jhānas using white kasiṇa as an object prior to starting a new kasiṇa.

NILA (BROWN / BLACK / BLUE) KASIṆA

The "nila" kasiṇa is a color likened to brown, blue, black, or a combination of the three. You may find that you have an affinity with one of these colors or the blended color of nila. Nila is based on the blue-black of black head hair or the color of bile from the thirty-two-body-parts meditation. If neither of these is the right color for you, then use an object in nature. We found that a color closest to those found on or in the human body was best for us.

Once again, undertake each jhāna using nila kasiṇa as an object until you attain the five masteries for each jhāna. Discern the appropriate jhāna factors with the wisdom eye in the bhavanga after each meditation period in each successive jhāna. When the five jhāna masteries are achieved, approach and cultivate the next jhāna as discussed earlier in this chapter in the "Meditative Procedure for Each Kasiṇa in the Material Jhānas" section. When you have successfully attained jhāna mastery in the fourth jhāna using nila kasiṇa as an object, you are ready for yellow kasiṇa.

YELLOW KASIṆA

The Venerable Pa Auk Sayadaw usually suggests that students use their urine as the yellow color for yellow kasiṇa. If this works, great. If not, then find a yellow flower or some other object in nature that has the color you feel intuitively to be the proper yellow kasiṇa color for this meditation. You can confirm that you have located the correct shade of yellow when you can easily see it for an extended period of time with eyes shut.

Proceed through each of the four jhānas using white kasiṇa as an object, with its corresponding jhāna factors. After completing all four jhānas using white kasiṇa, develop nila kasiṇa. Next, pass through each jhāna with its appropriate jhāna factors using nila kasiṇa as an object. Check the bhavanga with the wisdom eye after each jhāna to ensure that the proper jhāna factors were present.

Next, focus on the yellow kasiṇa until the first jhāna factors (vitakka, vicāra, pīti, sukha, and ekaggatā) arise. When concentration is strong enough, awareness is drawn into first jhāna using yellow kasiṇa as an object. Proceed with each of the four jhānas as with the prior kasiṇas, gaining the five masteries with each jhāna. Once the five jhāna masteries are attained with the fourth jhāna using yellow kasiṇa as an object, move to red kasiṇa.

RED KASIṆA

Next, seek a shade of red that intuitively feels like the right red color for a meditative object. The Venerable Pa Auk Sayadaw recommends using the color of the student's blood, as seen in the thirty-two-body-parts meditation. If the color of your blood does not easily become the color red for the kasiṇa meditation, you can find the proper color in nature—possibly a flower. There is no logical way to know the right shade of red. When you see the correct red for this meditation, you will know it.

As before, take the red color as your meditative object. See it when your eyes are closed in the same way as the colors white, nila, and yellow for those kasiṇas. If the red color fades before becoming independently stable, open your eyes to observe the red being used for the kasiṇa color. When you can see the red color with eyes closed, resume the meditation period. Once the red color has become the kasiṇa, proceed as before with expanding the red kasiṇa. Follow the same pattern as with the prior kasiṇas. When you have attained the five jhāna masteries for all four jhānas using red kasiṇa as an object, develop earth kasiṇa.

EARTH KASIṆA

We are now moving from color kasiṇas to kasiṇas based on the elements. We speculate that, while the color-kasiṇa meditations are based on body parts and purify various energies and perceptions of the body, the elements-kasiṇa meditations purify perception of the elements that make up the other aspect of materiality—our environment.

In preparing for earth kasiṇa, find dirt whose color represents the image of earth to you. (Note: this is earth as in dirt, not as in the image of the globe that floats in space.) If you want, collect a small amount of this dirt in a container. Alternatively, you can draw a circle on the ground outside and gaze at it for some minutes to imprint the visual image of earth. Initially, observe the dirt with open eyes. Eventually, you need to hold the image of earth independently as a meditative object when your eyes are closed. The image is then the meditative object for earth kasiṇa. As you progress through the remaining kasiṇas, the image of a kasiṇa is the meditative object for the particular kasiṇa. This prepares you to hold increasingly subtle kasiṇas as objects, as well as even more subtle meditative objects found in the immaterial jhānas.

When you can see and hold the earth image as a meditative object, earth-kasiṇa meditation begins. With time, the jhāna factors arise for the first jhāna, and the earth kasiṇa becomes stable and energized independently. Proceed to expand the earth kasiṇa to cover the entire world, including you. Allow your meditative attention to fall upon a small point on the expanded earth-kasiṇa and, through this spot, enter first jhāna, following the same progression as with the prior kasiṇas. Proceed through each of the first four jhānas following the same progression as with the prior kasiṇas. Complete each of the first through fourth jhānas to the point of the five jhāna masteries, using earth kasiṇa as an object. You are then ready for water kasiṇa.

WATER KASIṆA

Observe a bowl of water to develop water kasiṇa as a meditative object. When you can discern the water with eyes closed, take it as the object of meditation. If, while you are meditating, the object slips away, resume staring at the bowl of water with open eyes to recapture its image as a meditative object.

When you begin to perceive water with eyes closed, water becomes the focus of meditation until it becomes a kasiṇa. The five jhāna factors arise. Proceed to expand the water kasiṇa to cover the entire world, including you. Allow your meditative attention to fall upon a small point on the expanded water kasiṇa and, through this spot, enter first jhāna, following the same progression as with the prior kasiṇas. When you have attained the five jhāna masteries in each of the first, second, third, and fourth jhānas using water kasiṇa as an object, you are ready for fire kasiṇa.

FIRE KASIṆA

To obtain fire as an object of meditation, use a candle or some other small flame. Observe the flame open-eyed. Even though fire moves, it is possible to see it as a stable image with eyes closed. If you cannot see the object with eyes closed, return to observing the fire open-eyed. Once you can clearly see the object as a kasiṇa with eyes closed and the five jhāna factors have arisen, the fire kasiṇa appears stable and energized. Expand the fire kasiṇa as before, to include the entire world as well as you. Again, allow the meditative attention to fall naturally upon a small point on the expanded fire kasiṇa. Take this spot as the meditative object, drawing awareness into first jhāna. When you have attained the five jhāna masteries in the first jhāna using fire kasiṇa as an object, proceed with the kasiṇa-jhāna progression outlined above. Once you have attained the five jhāna masteries for second, third, and fourth jhānas using fire kasiṇa as an object, proceed with developing wind kasiṇa.

WIND KASIṆA

Taking wind as an object is difficult to understand conceptually. This is why cultivating the prior elements' kasiṇas is helpful. First, find a place where wind is blowing. Wind can be observed in a window, doorway, or outside blowing in bushes or trees. You can also feel the wind on your skin. If you can see an image of wind in your mind's eye, that can be taken as an object.

Take wind as the object of meditation. Wind becomes a kasiṇa. As the jhāna factors arise, the kasiṇa becomes stable and energized. Expand this energized kasiṇa until it fills the entire world, including you. When this expanded wind kasiṇa is stable, the meditative attention is drawn to a small point on the expanded kasiṇa. When the jhāna factors are of sufficient strength, awareness is drawn into first jhāna. The five jhāna masteries for first jhāna need to be obtained before moving on to second jhāna using wind kasiṇa as an object. The steps for the subsequent jhānas are outlined above.

Once you have attained the five jhāna masteries of the first, second, third, and fourth jhānas using wind kasiṇa as an object, proceed to light kasiṇa.

LIGHT KASIṆA

The object for this kasiṇa is light. To obtain light as a meditative object, observe light streaming through a window or doorway. Focus on the beam of light but not the particles that the light catches in the air. When clear morning sun is available, you can use the sun disc as a light-kasiṇa object. Other times, the sunlight that shines between tree branches or leaves may be suitable to use as a light-kasiṇa object. When closing your eyes, observe what remains as light. When you can detect light with eyes closed, take light as the meditative object. As the jhāna factors arise, light becomes a kasiṇa. With further meditation, the light kasiṇa becomes stable and independently energized. If the stable light kasiṇa does not expand on its own, expand it to cover the entire world, including you. When this expanded light kasiṇa is stable, the meditative attention falls upon a small point on the expanded light kasiṇa. When all the jhāna factors are sufficiently strong and the time is ripe, awareness is drawn into first jhāna. Follow the progression outlined above to obtain the five jhāna masteries for the second, third, and fourth jhānas using light kasiṇa as an object. This includes checking the bhavanga with the wisdom eye for the corresponding jhāna factors after exiting each jhāna.

When the five jhāna masteries have been obtained for the first, second, third, and fourth jhānas using light kasiṇa as an object, proceed to space kasiṇa.

SPACE KASIṆA

When we observe the stars, what we see between them is space. This can then be used as the basis for the space kasiṇa as an object. Another option is to hold a round circle against a clear sky. Pay attention to the space within the circle. Space is then held as a meditative object with eyes closed. As the jhāna factors arise, space becomes a kasiṇa. Continue with meditation on the space kasiṇa. When the jhāna factors and meditative concentration are sufficiently strong, the kasiṇa becomes stable and independently energized. Expand the space kasiṇa to cover the entire world, including you. After the expanded space kasiṇa stabilizes, the meditative attention shifts to a small point on the expanded space kasiṇa. In time, awareness enters first jhāna. Once the five jhāna masteries are obtained in the first jhāna using space kasiṇa as an object, follow the progression outlined in the "Meditative Procedure for Each Kasiṇa in the Material Jhānas" kasiṇa section to gain the five jhāna masteries for the second, third, and fourth jhānas using space kasiṇa as an object.

Although still in the material realm, space kasiṇa is approaching the immaterial realms / jhānas. There is a qualitative difference in the progression of kasiṇas, as each new kasiṇa is more refined, subtle, and delicate as a meditative object. You can see this, for example, from the fact that earth is much more dense than space. With each lighter and subtler kasiṇa, your localized consciousness is being refined and purified, which prepares your awareness to approach the immaterial realms of the upper jhānas.

The use of the kasiṇas as objects of meditation is another example of the Buddha's genius. We found that as we progressed through all ten kasiṇas, everywhere we looked around us became a trigger for the pristine awareness of the jhānas. The colors of the world, as well as the images of the elements, became supports to ongoing practice and continuity.

The "Base" Meditation Object and "Recharging" Concentration

During practice of the kasiṇas, for some people, the "base" meditative object sometimes shifts from the ānāpāna nimitta to the white kasiṇa. This is the object that you use as your "home base" to launch into high-level meditative objects. You also use it as your object while you are moving around. The Venerable Pa Auk Sayadaw instructs that you can make this shift and use white kasiṇa as the object while moving around in the world, or continue to use the ānāpāna nimitta as the base meditative object when you are eating, walking, and so on—whichever works better for you.

It can be helpful to use white kasiṇa as a base because the earth kasiṇa will be used repeatedly in the upper immaterial jhānas to access the base of boundless space (the fifth jhāna). While it is possible to go straight to earth kasiṇa, for most people white kasiṇa is an easier starting point, given its similarity to the ānāpāna nimitta and its ability to be seen even while moving around, walking, eating, and so on. Because earth kasiṇa is difficult to take as a base for many reasons, including its darker color, it is not recommended. The ānāpāna nimitta is another alternative; however, it begins to feel somewhat gross compared to the white kasiṇa at this point in the practice, which for some meditators makes white kasiṇa more useful.

Stephen found that he preferred to use the ānāpāna nimitta as a meditative base while walking, eating, and the like. When he sat for formal meditation, white kasiṇa arose naturally and provided easy access to earth kasiṇa. Tina found that the white kasiṇa arose naturally as an ongoing base at this point. However, over the many days of progressing through all the lower jhānas and kasiṇas, it was beneficial for her to return to the ānāpāna nimitta periodically to "charge up" the concentration.

Especially before moving on from one kasiṇa to another, it is important to have strong concentration. Therefore, returning to a meditation period with the ānāpāna nimitta as the object can be worthwhile and even prevent the progression from wobbling. Because the ānāpāna nimitta has the ever-present physical sensation of the breath, it is always easily accessible. Alternately, when you are undertaking a sitting period and progressing through several jhānas as you move to the higher kasiṇas, spending a few extra minutes in the first jhāna with ānāpāna nimitta can also create the jhāna "rocket fuel" necessary to maintain a solid progression.

We have now reviewed all the meditative practices through the fourth material jhāna. It is time to continue our journey into the four upper jhānas—the immaterial states that provide gateways to direct perception of the space that holds all materiality, the boundless consciousness that holds all space, a realm in which absolutely no thing is present, and that which is beyond all of these.

6

Immaterial Jhānas Five through
Eight and Related Practices

FOR AWARENESS to be absorbed into an immaterial jhāna is
among the most delicate of Buddhist practices and subtle meditations. The realms traversed are breathtaking in their vastness
and sheer depth of being: infinite space, unbounded consciousness, no-thing-ness, and that which is beyond. This is the terrain
presented here. The objects of meditation in these immaterial
realms are too insubstantial for imagination. Fortunately, they
can be experienced directly. The four immaterial jhānas are:

1. the base of boundless space (the fifth jhāna)
2. the base of boundless consciousness (the sixth jhāna)
3. the base of nothingness (the seventh jhāna)
4. the base of neither perception nor nonperception (the
   eighth jhāna)

In some texts, these meditations are not referred to as "jhānas"
because they are thought not to be true absorptions. Rather, it
is thought that they are actual, objective, nonmaterial (form-
less) realms that are accessed by awareness through the gateway

of the meditative object. The laserlike concentration developed in the lower jhānas and kasiṇas becomes the "key" to opening these gateways to the immaterial realms. Our experience was that they do indeed experientially feel more like immaterial realms than like meditative absorptions. However, because there is a progression of practice and for ease of language, we will refer to them primarily as immaterial jhānas and only occasionally as immaterial states or realms.

If you are able to attain the five jhāna masteries for each of the first four material jhānas using each of the ten kasiṇas as an object, the teacher may next direct you to the immaterial jhānas. When we taught with the Venerable Pa Auk Sayadaw on a retreat at the Forest Refuge, we learned that he sometimes directs students to the four elements meditation after they complete the first through fourth jhānas. He does not instruct everyone to go on to the upper jhānas. The direction on which way to proceed is based on a combination of the student's meditative ability and capacity, the student's intention in practice, and the remaining retreat time available. Attainment of the fourth jhāna provides a solid level of concentration with which to undertake the vipassanā practice. However, the Sayadaw instructed us that undertaking vipassanā with the power of all eight jhānas was most desirable in order to achieve the greatest depth and thoroughness of insight.

In completing the kasiṇa meditations, the meditator discovers and utilizes each of the ten kasiṇas as a meditative object for each material jhāna. Each successive kasiṇa, as the object for accessing the material jhānas, is lighter in appearance and more delicately subtle in its essence. Those who complete these practices have spent a minimum of three uninterrupted hours in each of the four material jhānas for each of the ten kasiṇas. Usually, several attempts have been made before time mastery is achieved.

This is an enormous amount of time to spend fully absorbed in the jhānas and in access concentration leading to absorption.

The meditative concentration has become stronger and increasingly subtle, focused, and laserlike. Also, moving from kasiṇa to kasiṇa and developing the specific jhāna factors for each of the four material jhānas with each kasiṇa demands the development of tremendous meditative skill and flexibility of mind, and promotes a nearly continuous purification of mind. Building progressive concentration on this number of objects and attaining the five masteries in each provides a solid foundation from which to attempt access to the immaterial realms.

Most meditators going on to the immaterial jhānas will start by using white kasiṇa as the beginning object and then move to earth kasiṇa, which provides access to the base of boundless space. The jhāna factors for the fourth material jhāna (ekaggatā and upekkhā) remain the same for each of the immaterial jhānas. Once you have progressed through each of the material jhānas using this method and have attained the five jhāna masteries in each immaterial jhāna, you will use all the other kasiṇas to also progress through the immaterial jhānas, with the exception of space kasiṇa. Space kasiṇa cannot be used because of its relationship to the base of boundless space (the fifth jhāna). Space cannot be used as a kasiṇa to enter space as an immaterial state. The five jhāna masteries are also attained for each kasiṇa in each upper jhāna, as they were in the four material jhānas.

The kasiṇas used to experience the immaterial jhānas are in a different order than for the lower four material jhānas. The order of the kasiṇas is changed for the immaterial jhānas to continuously refine and purify the student's consciousness. As you can see, in this case, the kasiṇas progress from more dense to less dense, to make the transition easier and to increase the refinement as the practice progresses. The order of the kasiṇas in the immaterial jhānas is:

1. earth kasiṇa
2. water kasiṇa
3. fire kasiṇa

4. wind kasiṇa
5. nila kasiṇa
6. yellow kasiṇa
7. red kasiṇa
8. white kasiṇa
9. light kasiṇa

BASE OF BOUNDLESS SPACE (THE FIFTH JHĀNA)

Proceeding from the base meditative object of either the ānāpāna nimitta or the white kasiṇa, take earth kasiṇa as a meditative object. If earth kasiṇa is difficult to see as an object for first jhāna, return to white kasiṇa practice. Take white kasiṇa as a meditative object and cultivate the jhāna factors for first jhāna (vitakka, vicāra, pīti, sukha, and ekaggatā). Proceed through the first, second, third, and fourth jhānas using white kasiṇa as an object, remaining in each until you reach stability and attain the five jhāna masteries. At this point, stability in the lower four jhānas is likely to be established in thirty minutes or less.

When earth kasiṇa can be taken as a meditative object and the jhāna factors are cultivated, enter first jhāna. When stability is reached in first jhāna using earth kasiṇa as an object, move to second jhāna (with the jhāna factors of pīti, sukha, and ekaggatā) with earth kasiṇa as the meditative object. When second jhāna stabilizes, continue to third jhāna (with sukha and ekaggatā as the jhāna factors). When third jhāna has stabilized, move to fourth jhāna (with the jhāna factors of ekaggatā and upekkhā). Enter and experience stability in the fourth jhāna using earth kasiṇa as an object.

While in access concentration near fourth jhāna, using earth kasiṇa as an object, direct your awareness to the space the expanded earth kasiṇa occupies. This is sometimes accomplished by seeing either minute holes in the earth kasiṇa or an edge of the earth kasiṇa—a seam where space and the earth kasiṇa meet.

Stephen found applying attention to the edge of the earth kasiṇa easier. Tina found the holes method easier. By focusing on either the small holes in the kasiṇa or the edge of the kasiṇa, direct your meditative attention to the space the earth kasiṇa occupies, by seeing either the holes or the seam where the kasiṇa and space meet. By focusing on the space the kasiṇa occupies and withdrawing attention from the earth kasiṇa, the earth kasiṇa is "removed."

The manner in which the earth kasiṇa leaves the space is not something to which you pay any attention. Have confidence that when space is effectively taken as a meditative object, the earth kasiṇa is not present. The important aspect at this point of the meditation is that earth kasiṇa is removed, leaving the space it formerly occupied. Next, direct the subtle awareness of space to its full vastness. This entire, all-encompassing space holds the infinite universe, including you.

When the jhāna factors of ekaggatā and upekkhā are strong and the bright jhāna energy is sufficiently concentrated, awareness focuses on a small spot in the unending expanded space. There is a spot that for some reason draws the attention quite naturally and easily. This small spot in the field of space then becomes the meditative object.

With sufficient time meditating on the "attention spot" in the field of unending space, awareness is drawn into full absorption in the base of boundless space (the fifth jhāna). The base of boundless space is the source of unending, unbounded, unlimited space in an immaterial realm. The experience of absorption into the base of boundless space is quite exquisite and qualitatively far more refined than the fourth jhāna of space kasiṇa. This is the space in which all objects in the material realm appear. Perhaps we can conceptually liken it to the canvas of life on which each brushstroke of life appears. It is a very profound experience.

As with the other jhānas, achieve the five masteries of this jhāna before moving to the base of boundless consciousness (the sixth jhāna) as a meditative object. Jhāna mastery includes one meditation period of three continuous hours of uninterrupted absorption in the base of boundless space. This is likely to take several attempts before the time mastery is achieved. The immaterial jhānas are a purer energy than the material jhānas. The refinement and purification of mind in the upper jhānas is a very intense experience. Until this purification is complete at the level of the base of boundless space, you will not be able to access the base of boundless consciousness. When the five jhāna masteries have been attained in the base of boundless space, you can proceed to attempt access to the base of boundless consciousness.

BASE OF BOUNDLESS CONSCIOUSNESS (THE SIXTH JHĀNA)

Proceeding from the base object of either the ānāpāna nimitta or the white kasiṇa, take earth kasiṇa as a meditative object and enter the first, second, third, and fourth jhānas using earth kasiṇa as an object. Expand earth kasiṇa as before to encompass the entire world. At this point, the jhāna factors of ekaggatā and upekkhā are present, as is true in the fourth jhāna and all the immaterial jhānas.

As before, direct the meditative attention to the space the earth kasiṇa occupies, either by seeing tiny holes in the earth kasiṇa or by focusing on the edge of the earth kasiṇa where it meets space. Remove the earth kasiṇa, and the new object of the base of boundless space arises.

Once again taking boundless space as a meditative object, meditate upon the awareness of unending space, in its full boundlessness and vastness. Next, allow the meditative attention to be drawn to a particular small spot in boundless space. When meditative concentration, upekkhā, and ekaggatā are of sufficient strength, awareness becomes fully absorbed into the base of boundless space (the fifth jhāna).

Direct attention to the consciousness that holds bound-less space as its object. An object such as the consciousness of boundless space is very difficult to speak about or imagine as a concept. Once the absorption into the base of boundless space (the fifth jhāna) has occurred, taking the consciousness of boundless space as a meditative object is subtle, yet apparent and somehow possible.

Naturally, the universal awareness that holds unending space as its object is a very subtle object itself, while also being very refined. When a meditator is at this point in the jhāna practice, the consciousness of the base of boundless space can indeed be taken as an object.

Take the consciousness that holds the base of boundless space as an object. The consciousness holding this object is by its nature infinite. As before in the fifth jhāna, this consciousness hold-ing boundless space is stabilized during meditation. The jhāna factors of ekaggatā and upekkhā are held until they are of the necessary strength. Once the consciousness holding boundless, unending space is known as the meditative object, and ekaggatā and upekkhā are strong, the attention can hold the entirety of this consciousness. Concentration and one-pointedness deepen and stabilize on this extremely subtle meditative object.

When ripe, awareness is drawn into full absorption in the base of boundless consciousness (the sixth jhāna). This bound-less, unending consciousness contains the infinite space that, ultimately, contains all materiality. This is the consciousness of the totality. Everything is contained within the one conscious-ness here, and this one consciousness pervades everywhere end-lessly. It is an undivided wholeness. The purification of mind facilitated by full absorption into the base of boundless con-sciousness that holds all space is profound.

As with the prior jhānas, the five jhāna masteries must be attained in the base of boundless consciousness before it is com-pleted. Once you have completed all five masteries in the sixth jhāna, including a single three-hour uninterrupted absorption in the base of boundless consciousness, proceed to the base of nothingness.

BASE OF NOTHINGNESS
(THE SEVENTH JHĀNA)

The object for the base of nothingness is the absence of the consciousness of boundless space. So, in effect, the new object is the absence of the object used for the sixth jhāna. Go through the first four jhānas using earth kasiṇa. If earth kasiṇa is difficult to take as a meditative object, begin with white kasiṇa and follow the proper steps to establish each of the first four jhānas using white kasiṇa as an object. Remain in each of the first four jhānas using white kasiṇa as an object until stable.

If you can easily see earth kasiṇa with eyes closed, then proceed accordingly through the first four jhānas using earth kasiṇa as an object. Remain in the four lower jhānas in earth kasiṇa only long enough to establish stability, perhaps five to ten minutes each. Then reestablish the base of boundless space by removing the earth kasiṇa and entering absorption here. Again, take the consciousness of the fifth jhāna, the base of boundless space, as an object and allow full absorption into the sixth jhāna to arise.

Stay in the sixth jhāna long enough to reach stability. Stability in the immaterial jhānas takes longer than in the lower four jhānas, as the upper jhānas are much more refined. When you are stable in the base of boundless consciousness, take up the base of nothingness by focusing on the absence of the consciousness of boundless space. Two mind moments do not arise simultaneously. When the consciousness of the base of boundless space is present, the base of boundless consciousness is absent. And, when the base of boundless consciousness is present, then the consciousness of the base of boundless space is absent. That absence of consciousness of the base of boundless space is used as the object for the seventh jhāna.

The nothingness of this immaterial state, the seventh jhāna, is complete, unending emptiness. Emptiness is a rich fullness of no identity and no thing. It is "no-thing-ness." Usually, with forms (such as thoughts, people, and objects), there are many ways that we mark the forms with identity. We can have a certain feeling about or relationship to a particular form. In the base of nothingness, all sense of any form or structure, as well as any markers of identity, are gone. This is a dramatic shift. The base of boundless consciousness is a fullness that contains the immensity of infinite space, which ultimately holds all materiality. In contrast, the base of nothingness is the utter void, the "dazzling darkness."

This is not an unpleasant jhāna. There is a sense of pristine purity, of freedom, here. Despite being no-thing-ness, there is a sense of presence—a deep, still, pervasive peace. It is the experience of no-thing from which all materiality (consciousness and space) can arise and be supported.

When the absence of the consciousness of the fifth jhāna of boundless space can be held, it becomes the meditative object. This may require many attempts, as the object is so fine it can easily slip away. This is an object that is delicately held, like holding gauze up to the sky. When ready, the object becomes stable and attention focuses on a particular spot within this nothingness. The spot is not actually within nothingness; it is within the heart base. This is a technical specification that the beginning meditator need not understand. However, the perception of a specific location in primordial nothingness allows awareness to attentively rest and eventually be absorbed.

Once awareness is deeply concentrated on the absence of the consciousness of boundless space, and the jhāna factors of ekaggatā and upekkhā are strongly present, awareness is drawn into full absorption in this immaterial state. As with the prior jhānas, continue with this jhāna until the five jhāna masteries have been achieved, including a single three-hour uninterrupted absorption in this jhāna.

With each of the immaterial jhānas, a tremendous amount of purification occurs. The meditator's mind stream is directly entering and being suffused by the no-thing-ness from which boundless consciousness arises. For awareness to be fully absorbed in these realms, beyond access concentration, is indescribable. These are sublime realms unimaginable to the thinking mind. Until these immaterial states are deeply known experientially, the student must take their existence on faith in the Buddha and the jhāna teachers.

After attaining the five jhāna masteries in the base of nothingness, you are ready for the next immaterial jhāna: the base of neither perception nor nonperception.

BASE OF NEITHER PERCEPTION NOR NONPERCEPTION (THE EIGHTH JHĀNA)

Take earth kasiṇa as the meditative object. If earth kasiṇa is difficult to begin with as a meditative object, start with white kasiṇa. Develop white kasiṇa as before through the first four jhānas using white kasiṇa as an object, until stable in each jhāna.

When you can take earth kasiṇa as a meditative object, develop first jhāna. When stable in first jhāna, develop and enter second jhāna using earth kasiṇa as an object. As stability is obtained in second jhāna, third jhāna is developed and stabilized, and then fourth jhāna. After achieving stability in fourth jhāna using earth kasiṇa, go through the process of removing earth kasiṇa as the object. Again, focus on either minute holes in the earth kasiṇa or the edge of the earth kasiṇa.

As before, remove earth kasiṇa and take the space that earth kasiṇa formerly occupied as a meditative object. When the jhāna factors of ekaggatā and upekkhā are strong, shift attention to a small spot in boundless space and focus on this as the object until awareness is drawn into the base of boundless space.

The consciousness holding the base of boundless space will become stable as a meditative object, and the jhāna factors of ekaggatā and upekkhā will become strong. When ripe, awareness is drawn into full absorption in the sixth jhāna, the base of boundless consciousness. Upon exiting the sixth jhāna, take the absence of the consciousness of the base of boundless space as the meditative object.

Hold the absence of the consciousness of the base of boundless space as a meditative object, until the jhāna factors of ekaggatā and upekkhā become strong. When concentration is ripe, the base of nothingness draws awareness into full absorption in the seventh jhāna. Upon exiting the seventh jhāna, proceed toward the eighth jhāna—the base of neither perception nor nonperception.

Now take the consciousness of the base of nothingness as the meditative object. Shift attention away from the base of nothingness and focus on the consciousness holding nothingness. This "consciousness of nothing" is the container in which nothingness is held. This is an even finer gauzelike object. To hold an object as subtle and fine as this, the sense of "me" must be almost completely transparent. Taking the consciousness of the base of nothingness as a meditative object is like holding a spiderweb to the sky. It is a very delicate, exquisitely fragile object of awareness. Only a purified, jhāna-energized awareness can hold the object of the base of neither perception nor nonperception.

Take the consciousness of the base of nothingness as a meditative object. With time, the jhāna factors of ekaggatā and upekkhā become strong. With prolonged meditation, awareness is eventually drawn into full absorption in the base of neither perception nor nonperception, the eighth jhāna.

This jhāna cannot begin to be imagined or conceptualized. While being outside perception and nonperception, this realm contains both and neither—at the same time! It is a direct experience of nondual awareness. There is neither perception nor nonperception in this immaterial realm. This immaterial state is beyond a sense of mentality; the normal, thinking mind absolutely cannot grasp it. Thinking cannot be present here, not even in access concentration. If it arises, the base of neither perception nor nonperception wafts away, like a wisp of smoke.

The first time each of us experienced this realm, it was unimaginably spectacular. For Tina, it was so intense that she could tolerate only a few minutes the first few times before awareness settled and there was a complete surrender to its purification and subtlety. Stephen was knocked out of the jhāna after about one and a half hours. His awareness could not have remained in the base of neither perception nor nonperception one second longer at that time. This was less than was needed for jhāna mastery. Yet even the first experience of this jhāna was akin to being completely reborn as a new, innocent, pure being.

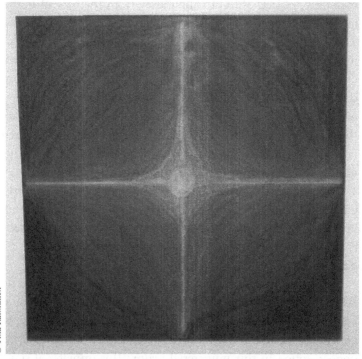

© *Tina Rasmussen*

Essence of the Eighth Jhāna. *Drawing by Tina Rasmussen.*

Once the five jhāna masteries are attained, including one un-interrupted meditation period of three hours, the eighth jhāna is complete. Proceed to the other kasiṇas.

ORDER OF KASIṆAS THROUGH THE IMMATERIAL JHĀNAS

The kasiṇas in the immaterial jhānas are completed in the following order:

1. earth kasiṇa
2. water kasiṇa
3. fire kasiṇa
4. wind kasiṇa
5. nila kasiṇa
6. yellow kasiṇa
7. red kasiṇa
8. white kasiṇa
9. light kasiṇa

Take up the remaining eight kasiṇas (space kasiṇa is excluded) as the object of entry to the four immaterial jhānas. Use each kasiṇa as the object through the four immaterial jhānas, progressing through the four immaterial jhānas of the base of boundless space, the base of boundless consciousness, the base of nothingness, and the base of neither perception nor non-perception. Achieve the five jhāna masteries with each of the immaterial jhānas through each kasiṇa, including one meditation period of three hours in each immaterial jhāna with each kasiṇa.

Begin by taking the kasiṇa as an object into first jhāna. Do this as quickly as the jhāna can be stabilized using that kasiṇa as an object. Then take the specific kasiṇa through the second, third, and fourth jhānas, also one at a time. As before, upon exiting jhāna, check the bhavanga with the wisdom eye to confirm that the requisite jhāna factors are present. Over time, you can move through each lower jhāna in a matter of a few minutes.

Once all lower jhānas are completed with the specific kasiṇa, access each upper jhāna as described with earth kasiṇa. Complete the first four jhānas using the particular kasiṇa and then either see tiny holes in the kasiṇa or focus on the edge where the kasiṇa touches space. Then remove the kasiṇa to reveal the space that holds it as the base of boundless space. Proceed as previously described through the four upper jhānas.

The element (earth, water, fire, and air) kasiṇas are completed first to purify and loosen your connection to the elements in your body and all materiality. Then the color kasiṇas are completed, purifying your attachment to bodily colors. This, too, is done to refine your consciousness for the light kasiṇa, which is the most refined of the kasiṇas in the immaterial jhānas. Using the light kasiṇa as an entry point leading to the delicacy of the eighth jhāna of neither perception nor nonperception is an exquisitely refined and subtle experience.

The purification that occurs in the immaterial upper jhānas is delicate yet very concentrated and intense. You must be willing to allow the purity to penetrate your entire being and life. We can attest that when the five jhāna masteries are attained, using the final light kasiṇa and completing the final jhāna of the base of neither perception nor nonperception, there is a deep and profound knowing of never being the same person again. The purification continues working on us and later manifests in our lives in unexpected ways that change our beliefs, opinions, habits, and behavior.

More important, this practice has altered the ongoing experiential awareness of the manifestation of all that we see—from our own body-minds to the material world around us. Even now, years later, we can experience at any moment the profundity of awareness as it is experienced in the eighth jhāna. There is an ongoing perception that all materiality manifests from the mystery of the unconditioned, down through the immaterial realms, into the material realms, and eventually appearing as materiality—as the words on this page and your perception of them, as the breath that we are breathing as we write these words. Even when the daily experience of jhāna absorption is past, this visceral knowing remains, affecting and informing each moment of experience and its relationship to the mystery.

We have now traversed the most delicate of meditations. With this very pristine, refined concentration and purification as a foundation, we next move into the protective meditations, which prepare the meditator to eventually undertake the vipassanā practice.

7

The Sublime Abidings and Protective Meditations

WHEN YOU have completed the jhāna progression through the eighth jhāna, the next stage of practice is to complete the sublime abidings and protective meditations.

The four sublime abidings (*bramavihāras*) consist of the following meditation subjects:

1. mettā (loving-kindness)
2. karuṇā (compassion)
3. muditā (joy)
4. upekkhā (equanimity)

The four protective meditations consist of the following meditation subjects:

1. mettā (loving-kindness)
2. recollection of the Buddha
3. foulness meditation
4. recollection of death

The primary purpose of all these practices is to provide a solid base of support as the meditator progresses toward the insight practice of vipassanā. Because the insights that arise in vipassanā are deeply uprooting to the sense of self and of materiality and mentality as they have been previously known, the experience can be destabilizing for a person's sense of "me." The protective meditations serve various purposes in stabilizing the meditator's practice and encouraging him or her to proceed in the face of this destabilization—the conflict between the world as we conceptually know it and the realization of things as they truly are.

The sublime abidings provide a sense of well-being to clear the meditator's karma with others and build the equanimity necessary for the uprooting and releasing that happens in vipassanā. The recollection of the Buddha provides inspiration and a direct feeling of connection to the Buddha as one who has completed this practice to its full fruition and whose teachings have guided millions of practitioners through the ages. The foulness meditation (meditation on a corpse) softens the meditator's attachment to him- or herself as the body. The recollection of death stimulates a sense of urgency regarding practice; it shows that there is no time to waste in realizing the truth because we never know when this life may end. Though these may sound very traditional to modern practitioners, they are well worth doing and offer us a variety of benefits as a foundation for vipassanā and may even be returned to as necessary during the vipassanā practice.

A secondary purpose of these practices is to continue deepening the faculty of concentration by providing additional meditation objects that can lead to various levels of concentration. With each of the above meditation subjects, the Venerable Pa Auk Sayadaw asks his students to obtain the following level of concentration:

- mettā (loving-kindness)—third jhāna
- karuṇā (compassion)—third jhāna
- muditā (joy)—third jhāna

- upekkhā (equanimity)—fourth jhāna
- recollection of the Buddha—access concentration
- foulness meditation—first jhāna
- recollection of death—access concentration

The first three sublime abidings are available only up to the third jhāna because they have an intrinsic sense of joy and happiness that is not present in the fourth jhāna. Upekkhā (equanimity) can be used as a meditative subject up to the fourth jhāna because the remaining jhāna factors in the fourth jhāna are one-pointedness and equanimity. These four objects of the sublime abidings build on one another sequentially beginning with mettā, so the culmination of this practice is the fourth jhāna in the practice of upekkhā.

With the additional three protective meditations beyond mettā, only access concentration or first jhāna is possible. For this reason, the Sayadaw encourages students to spend just one to two hours on this practice at a time so as not to dissipate the high concentration of the jhānas.

While completing these practices, you also must continue jhāna meditation for one sitting per day, completing up to the eighth jhāna. This ensures that the intensive jhāna-level concentration is available for use with these and other practices and does not dissipate over time.

Each of these practices is done by beginning with the ānāpāna nimitta or white kasiṇa as the object, up to the fourth jhāna. Because you have already completed a long period of time with the material and immaterial jhānas using the ānāpāna nimitta and the kasiṇas as primary objects, this is easy to do. Establishment of a minimum of the fourth jhāna using your ongoing "base" meditation object of the ānāpāna nimitta or white kasiṇa before beginning the sublime abidings and protective meditations ensures that you have powerful concentration at the start and makes it easier to establish the highest possible level of concentration on these new subjects.

Details of these meditation practices are outlined thoroughly in the Venerable Pa Auk Sayadaw's book *Knowing and Seeing* and thus will not be presented here. The sublime abidings (*bramavihāras*) are taught widely in North America and Europe, and the Venerable Pa Auk Sayadaw's instruction on the practice is similar, but with some variations.

Once the practitioner has completed the sublime abidings and protective meditations, she or he is ready to proceed to the four elements meditation and move toward the beginning of the vipassanā practice.

8

Four Elements Meditation

FOUR ELEMENTS MEDITATION is a critical practice to develop well. All students of the Venerable Pa Auk Sayadaw must develop this meditation to undertake the vipassanā portion of the Buddha's path. In this practice, we experientially learn and know that all that appears "real," including our own bodies, is comprised of a combination of the four elements. The belief in, and attachment to, the body becomes difficult to sustain after this practice is thoroughly experienced.

There are two ways in which a student undertakes the four elements meditation. For those who have completed the practices as outlined in this book, the four elements meditation is the next practice in the samatha sequence. Those students who can attain jhāna using the ānāpānasati meditation take up four elements meditation after the sublime abidings and protective meditations, discussed in the preceding chapter. The sublime abidings and protective meditations are undertaken to allow greater ease in facing the rigors of the kalāpa practice that are experienced as a result of the four elements meditation. The four elements meditation then serves as the bridge that completes the samatha practices and begins the vipassanā practice. Practitioners completing the samatha portion as outlined in this book would be considered "samatha yogis."

The Venerable Pa Auk Sayadaw indicates that if someone finds, after exhaustive effort, that she or he cannot progress through the jhānas beginning with ānāpānasati meditation, the student may be directed to try four elements meditation. (This is why our practice chart reflects the four elements as an alternate beginning point to ānāpānasati meditation.) These practitioners would be considered "vipassanā yogis" or "dry-insight yogis," as they are proceeding directly to the vipassanā practice.

The four elements meditation allows you to experience your body as being composed entirely of a blend of the four elements. It is not possible to attain jhāna using the four elements as an object, as they are objects of momentary concentration. However, four elements meditation can lead to access concentration.

Four elements meditation in its later application is used to directly discern (see) and analyze rūpa-kalāpas. Rūpa-kalāpas are tiny subatomic particles that make up all objects in the world of materiality. We will not discuss using four elements meditation beyond the point of seeing kalāpas because that is the end of the samatha practice, which is the focus of this book.

Four Elements Meditation Instructions

The four elements are earth, water, fire, and air, with their associated characteristics.

1. earth element: hardness, roughness, heaviness, softness, smoothness, lightness
2. water element: flowing, cohesion
3. fire element: heat, coldness
4. air element: supporting, pushing

Pairing each element with its opposite allows an easier initial progression through the characteristics of each of the four elements. After learning the pairs in this way, you should then complete the four elements meditation in the traditional order. We present the characteristics below in an order that we believe is easier to learn. The progression we recommend first is:

1. hardness, softness
2. roughness, smoothness
3. heaviness, lightness
4. flowing, cohesion
5. heat, cold
6. supporting, pushing

To begin the four elements practice, if you have previously completed the jhāna practice, you should use white kasiṇa as an object to progress through the first, second, third, and fourth jhānas. If you have not completed the jhāna practice, you can proceed to start the four elements meditation directly.

In either case, begin by seeking all hardness in your body. Examples of hardness are teeth, bones, and nails. Experientially locate each area of hardness in your body. When you can find and simultaneously hold all areas of hardness in your body without division or distraction, begin searching your body for softness, ignoring hardness entirely at this time.

Softness is everything that is not hardness. Literally, your experience in the body during this pairing is either of hardness or of softness when evaluating just these two characteristics of the earth element. If you can easily hold hardness, you can shift your attention to everywhere else in your body to find all that is softness. Then alternate between hardness and softness until you can discern and feel each in literally an instant. Then hold hardness and softness distinctly and simultaneously.

Next, examine the characteristics of roughness and smoothness. An example of roughness might be the tough skin on the bottom of your feet. Discover and experience all roughness in your body, until you can feel it at once everywhere.

You can find smoothness by running your tongue over your lip, as one example. The tongue also feels quite smooth on the teeth. Seek smoothness everywhere in your body. Then alternate between roughness and smoothness. When you can find roughness and smoothness quickly, both separately and simultaneously, advance to heaviness and lightness.

You can feel heaviness where the bottom of your body (that is, legs, feet, or buttocks) touches the meditation cushion, chair, or floor. Once you can know this everywhere in the body at once, shift your meditative awareness to lightness. One example of how lightness might be experienced is the hair on your arms. Continue to explore your body, searching everywhere for lightness. When you can clearly sense lightness and heaviness throughout the body, sense them by quickly shifting from one to the other. Then hold heaviness and lightness simultaneously and distinctly.

Flowing and cohesion are the next characteristics to look for in your body. You can sense flowing as the blood or other liquids moving throughout your body, for example. Detect all areas of flowing in the body. Feel each area of flowing at once before moving to cohesion. Cohesion is felt as how the body holds itself together. The various muscles, blood vessels, and organs remarkably stay within the skin of this body. Feel cohesion everywhere in the body at once. Then alternate between flowing and cohesion. When you can experience each of these completely in one instant, shift to feeling both of these together distinctly and simultaneously.

Heat and cold need no explanation. It is fairly easy to find these characteristics in your body. Again, experience these by alternating one and then the other, until each can be distinctly experienced simultaneously with the other in an instant.

Supporting and pushing are a little tricky to find. Supporting is how the various organs are held in place by their location and other factors you discover. Likewise, you can feel pushing when your breath is drawn into your body with deep deliberation. The wind pushes in your lungs expanding the chest, allowing your body to breathe. Explore the body to find every area of supporting. Then, once all areas of supporting are found, shift attention to pushing, locating all places of pushing in the body. As you clearly discern these and learn to know them deeply, alternate attention from supporting to pushing and back again. Feel each characteristic as completely distinct from the other characteristic and then discern them simultaneously.

Once you can easily identify each characteristic in each of the four elements, proceed to locating these characteristics in the traditionally prescribed order.

ORDER OF CHARACTERISTICS OF EACH ELEMENT AS IN THE TRADITIONAL INSTRUCTIONS

After you have learned all the characteristics in the above order, begin to locate the characteristics of each element in the following order, as is done traditionally. Again, the order of the traditional instruction is:

1. earth element: hardness, roughness, heaviness, softness, smoothness, lightness
2. water element: flowing, cohesion
3. fire element: heat, cold
4. air element: supporting, pushing

Once you have sufficiently experienced all the characteristics separately, experience each group as an entire element. For instance, the characteristics of the water element are flowing and cohesion. Once you have learned these separately, sense them simultaneously in the body, holding them as the water element.

When you can experience each characteristic for each element, cycle through each element, feeling all its characteristics separately at once. When you can hold each element, with all its characteristics, proceed to run through the elements in order of earth, water, fire, and air. When you can distinctly feel each element in the body, cycle through all the elements to the point where you can do three complete rounds of all the elements in a minute, with each element being distinctly experienced. You are likely to experience the body as a combination of these elements, not as a distinct body. There is no part of the body that does not reflect one characteristic of an element. There comes a time when you can hold each element with its distinctness with all the other elements at once.

The Venerable Pa Auk Sayadaw then instructed us to use the wisdom eye to obtain a vantage point just above and behind the body, as if we were looking slightly down on our own body from right above and in back of the head. With continued deep meditation on the four elements, there develops a light, a kind of glow around the body. Do not shift your meditative attention to the glow but allow it to develop on its own. Our experience, at this point, was of seeing the entire body in its four elements as a white, cloudlike form. Despite the white, cloudlike form, continue to maintain meditative attention cycling through the four elements. Over time this white form begins to become crystal-like.

The white form transmutes into a perceived crystal body— your crystal body. Over time, the crystal body becomes brilliant in its glow and is perceived as diamond-hard. This diamondlike body begins to glow with a brilliant light, which expands in every direction. You can see the emanating light during meditation. At this time, the brilliant crystal body feels very clear and pure.

As with many of these practices, we were not sure what would happen when we started or what to expect. But, by staying true to the practice and maintaining awareness on the object, the practice did progress as described.

Variations on How and When to Do This Practice

In Stephen's case, because of physical issues, he undertook four elements meditation at the beginning before going on to the ānāpānasati practice. You can use the four elements meditation to balance the four elements and characteristics, should they be out of balance. For example, a meditator might seek softness or flowing in a part of the body that is stiff and painful. For Stephen, doing four elements meditation first enabled his bodily energies to smooth out before undertaking the ānāpānasati meditation. As mentioned earlier, in most cases the teacher will encourage students to do the ānāpānasati meditation first and, if they are not successful, to then proceed to the four elements practice.

In Tina's case, she completed the practices in the sequence given by the Venerable Pa Auk Sayadaw in his book *Knowing and Seeing*. If you are doing the four elements meditation in this way—that is, after having completed all of the jhānas, kasiṇas, related practices, and protective meditations—you should also continue practicing the jhānas up to the eighth jhāna during one meditation period each day to maintain a high level of jhāna concentration. If you have completed fourth jhāna, or even first jhāna, continue to do one sitting per day up to the highest jhāna obtained to maintain concentration. This makes for a powerful entry into the beginning of the vipassanā practice, starting with the four elements meditation. It ensures that the concentration developed over the many days, weeks, and months of practice is sustained and available to use in the vipassanā portion of the Buddhist path.

The four elements meditation is very different from jhāna practice, in that it is fast-moving and requires the use of momentary concentration rather than absorption. You will not experience absorption in doing the four elements meditation; rather, you use momentary concentration to develop a high level of access concentration. Practicing the jhānas at one sitting per day allows for a high level of concentration; then you can switch to doing the four elements meditation practice for the rest of the day.

RŪPA-KALĀPAS

Toward the end of the retreat with the Venerable Pa Auk Sayadaw, after spending some days on the four elements meditation and progressing to the crystal body, Tina started perceiving a vibrating sensation internally during meditation with eyes closed and externally with eyes open while moving around. This is common once the perception of the crystal body becomes stable, and it is seen in block form for at least thirty consecutive minutes of access concentration. At this point, the meditator is instructed to look for the space element in the transparent form of the crystal body.

As this practice progresses, the crystal body can suddenly break down into small particles called rūpa-kalāpas, which are the subatomic particles of materiality that comprise all matter. Seeing rūpa-kalāpas is the final stage of samatha practice before you begin analyzing the rūpa-kalāpas. Analyzing rūpa-kalāpas is the first stage of the vipassanā practice, according to the Buddha's teaching as presented by the Venerable Pa Auk Sayadaw.

In Tina's experience, seeing rūpa-kalāpas had a significant and permanent impact on her perception of materiality/physical reality. Having a direct experience of seeing everything one looks at (including one's own body) as moving subatomic particles alters the perception of "me" and of the substantiality of what we regard as "normal" reality. Stephen experienced a moment, a brief flash, of seeing rūpa-kalāpas. Due to the limited duration of his experience, it had less of an impact.

It is useful to remember that the samatha portion of the Buddhist path is traditionally described as the "purification of mind," while the vipassanā portion is described as the "purification of view." The internal purification of one's mind stream lays the groundwork for purifying the internal and external "view" of reality as we come to know it as it actually is rather than as the conditioned mind has taken it to be. Seeing, and later analyzing, rūpa-kalāpas is the beginning of seeing materiality as it actually is without the overlay of conceptual thought.

This completes the samatha meditations we learned under the guidance of the Venerable Pa Auk Sayadaw. Your experience may be slightly different from ours, given the unique nature of the solitary journey upon which we embark in the purification of mind offered by these ancient practices.

9

The Buddha as Our Role Model

WE BEGAN this book by describing the context of the jhānas as they were learned, practiced, and taught by the Buddha. It is appropriate that we end with this context as well.

Modern practitioners sometimes wonder whether the jhānas are necessary. Are they are still an important, or even an essential, aspect of practice? Or are they an extraneous form of meditation—not only unnecessary but also beyond the reach of most people? Meditators have debated these questions for thousands of years and are unlikely to resolve them soon, if ever. Thus, each of us needs to determine the answer to these questions for ourselves.

For us, the answer lies in the practice of the Buddha himself. If he is our role model, should we not follow the path that he not only taught but personally practiced throughout his life, even at the moment of death?

By following the Buddha's ingenious design and role modeling of the path of sīla, samatha, and vipassanā, we plant the seeds for an ever-deepening purification of mind, within which the wisdom of liberation can flower.

• • •

May you experientially know each step in the footprints of the Buddha on your path to realizing liberation.

Epilogue

In 1934, the boy Acinna was born in Leigh-Chaung village about one hundred miles northwest of Yangon, Myanmar. At the age of ten, he was ordained as a novice (*samanera*) in the Theravada Buddhist tradition in his village. Later, at the age of twenty, he was ordained as a full-fledged monk, a *bhikkhu*. As a *samanera* and as a *bhikkhu*, he was trained under the guidance of learned elder monks, completing the prestigious Dhamma-cariya examination in 1954 (the equivalent of a master's degree in Buddhist Pāli studies).

For the next eight years, he traveled throughout Myanmar to learn from various well-known Buddhist teachers. In 1964, he began "forest dwelling" (living a life of renunciation, dedicated to spiritual practice in the forest or jungle) in order to intensify his meditation practice. For the next sixteen years, he made forest dwelling his primary practice, living a simple life of intensive meditation and scriptural study.

In 1981, the Venerable Acinna received a message from the Venerable Aggapanna, the abbot of Pa Auk Forest Monastery at the time. The Venerable Aggapanna was dying and asked the

Venerable Acinna to look after the monastery. Five days later, the Venerable Aggapanna died, and the Venerable Acinna became known as the Venerable Pa Auk Tawya Sayadaw, the new abbot. Although he oversaw monastery operations, he spent most of his time in seclusion, meditating in a bamboo hut in the upper forest of the monastery grounds.

Foreign meditators began arriving at the monastery in the early 1990s, as the Sayadaw's reputation grew as a highly-attained meditator and an English-speaking abbot. In 1997, the Venerable Pa Auk Sayadaw wrote his magnum opus, the enormous five-volume tome in Burmese titled *The Practice That Leads to Nibbāna*, explaining the entire course of the Buddha's teaching in detail, supported by copious quotations from the texts in Pāli (in which he is fluent). In 1999, in public recognition of his achievements, the government of Myanmar bestowed upon him the title of "Highly Respected Meditation Teacher." In 1999, the Venerable Pa Auk Sayadaw wrote *Knowing and Seeing* (available in English), which is a condensed, 350-page version of this path of practice, including extensive instruction on the material and immaterial jhānas.

The monastery has since expanded to more than 800 full-time monastic and lay practitioners, four meditation halls, a library, a clinic, a hospital, and an almsgiving hall. The population sometimes now exceeds 1,500 people during festivals.

Meanwhile, in the United States, in 1976, four American friends established the Insight Meditation Society (IMS) in Barre, Massachusetts, after studying Theravada Buddhism in Southeast Asia. Joseph Goldstein, Jack Kornfield, Sharon Salzberg, and Jacqueline Schwartz studied with numerous teachers and brought these teachings (primarily focusing on insight meditation in the lineage of the Venerable Mahāsī Sayadaw) back to the West. Since they were some of the first Americans teaching Buddhism, the spread of the practices was gradual and sometimes slow. But with persistence and dedication, the sangha grew.[1]

In 1981, the Venerable Mahāsī Sayadaw, a well-known and respected Buddhist teacher, came to IMS to officially certify the center as an Insight Meditation Center in his tradition. In 1987, Jack Kornfield directed the purchase of the land for Spirit Rock Retreat Center in Woodacre, California.

Together Spirit Rock and IMS host tens of thousands of meditators annually, some completing retreats as long as two or three months. IMS and Spirit Rock continue to host the most respected Asian Theravada teachers, including the Venerable Pa Auk Sayadaw and many others.

At the writing of this book, the Venerable Pa Auk Sayadaw is more than seventy years old. He is now considered by many to be the leading Asian master teaching the jhāna practices, in addition to the insight practices of vipassanā. Now is the time to learn this ancient and worthy practice, before it is lost to obscurity.

When the Sayadaw was young, his teacher charged him with planting the seeds of the Buddha's teachings in the West. Despite his advancing age, he continues to travel around the world to offer these teachings, preserving them and passing them on.

SAMATHA

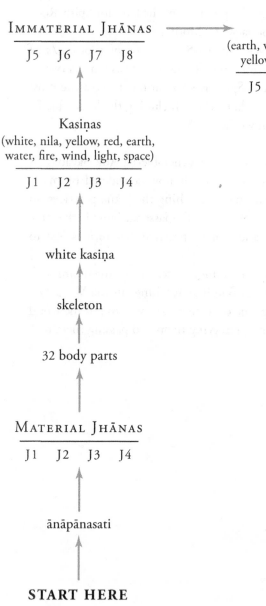

IMMATERIAL JHĀNAS ——→ Kasiṇas
(earth, water, fire, wind, nila,
yellow, red, white, light)

J5   J6   J7   J8

J5   J6   J7   J8

Kasiṇas
(white, nila, yellow, red, earth,
water, fire, wind, light, space)

J1   J2   J3   J4

Sublime Abidings

J1   J2   J3   J4

white kasiṇa

skeleton

32 body parts

MATERIAL JHĀNAS

J1   J2   J3   J4

ānāpānasati

START HERE
(in most cases)

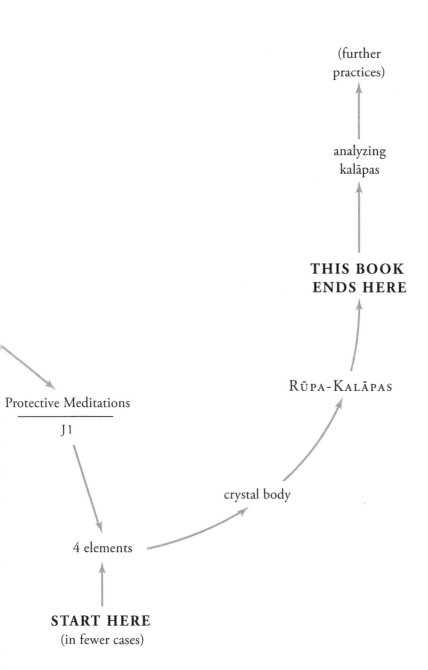

VIPASSANĀ

(further
practices)

analyzing
kalāpas

**THIS BOOK
ENDS HERE**

Rūpa-Kalāpas

Protective Meditations

J1

crystal body

4 elements

START HERE
(in fewer cases)

Notes

Chapter 1: History of the Jhānas

1. Ariyapariyesana Sutta, Majjhima Nikāya 26. *The Middle Length Discourses of the Buddha: A Translation of the Majjhima Nikāya,* trans., ed., and rev. Bhikkhu Ñāṇamoli and Bhikkhu Bodhi (Somerville, Mass.: Wisdom Publications, 1995), 253.
2. The *Visuddhimagga* is a treatise of Theravada Buddhism, in the form of a detailed practice manual. It was written in the fifth century as an organized compilation of the Buddha's teachings as found in the suttas of the Pāli Canon.
3. Mahasaccaka Sutta, Majjhima Nikāya 36. *Middle Length Discourses of the Buddha,* 332.
4. Ibid.
5. MahaParinibbāna Sutta, Dīgha Nikāya 16. *The Long Discourses of the Buddha: A Translation of the Dīgha Nikāya,* trans. Maurice Walshe (Somerville, Mass.: Wisdom Publications, 1995), 231.
6. Ibid.
7. Pa Auk Tawya Sayadaw, *Knowing and Seeing* (Kuala Lumpur, Malaysia: WAVE Publications, 2003). (Available for free download at www.paauk.org.)

Chapter 2: Samatha Practice

1. Saṃyutta Nikāya 45.8. *The Connected Discourses of the Buddha: A Translation of the Saṃyutta Nikāya,* trans. Bhikkhu Bodhi (Somerville, Mass.: Wisdom Publications, 2000), 1528.
2. Walpola Sri Rahula, *What the Buddha Taught* (New York: Grove Press, 1959).
3. From Dhammacakkappavattana Sutta, Saṃyutta Nikāya 56.11. *Connected Discourses of the Buddha,* 1843.

4. See Magga-vibhanga, Saṃyutta Nikāya 45.8. *Connected Discourses of the Buddha*, 1528. See also Mahasatipatthana Sutta, Dīgha Nikāya 22. *The Long Discourses of the Buddha: A Translation of the Dīgha Nikāya*, trans. Maurice Walshe (Somerville, Mass.: Wisdom Publications, 1995), 335.

5. Pa Auk Tawya Sayadaw, *Knowing and Seeing* (Kuala Lumpur, Malaysia: WAVE Publications, 2003), 42.

6. See Ahara Sutta, Saṃyutta Nikāya 46.51. *Connected Discourses of the Buddha*, 1597.

7. Bhadantacariya Buddhaghosa, *Visuddhimagga: The Path of Purification*, trans. Bhikkhu Ñāṇamoli (Seattle, Wash.: BPS Pariyatti, 1999), 125.

8. Ibid., 99.

9. Confidental conversation with a yogi in April, 2008.

10. Bhikkhu Bodhi, "Purification of Mind," *Buddhist Publication Society Newsletter*, cover essay no. 4 (Summer 1986), 2.

11. Amy Schmidt, *Knee Deep in Grace: The Extraordinary Life and Teaching of Dipa Ma* (Lake Junaluska, N.C.: Present Perfect Books, 2003).

12. Ajahn Chah, *Food for the Heart: The Collected Teachings of Ajhan Chah* (Somerville, Mass.: Wisdom Publications, 2003), 150.

13. Thanissaro Bhikkhu, "Pushing the Limits: Desire & Imagination in the Buddhist Path," Access to Insight, 2006, www.accesstoinsight.org/lib/authors/thanissaro/pushinglimits.html.

Chapter 3: Foundational Understandings

1. *The Connected Discourses of the Buddha: A Translation of the Saṃyutta Nikāya*, trans. Bhikkhu Bodhi (Somerville, Mass.: Wisdom Publications, 2000), 1270.

2. See Samannaphala Sutta, Dīgha Nikāya 2. *The Long Discourses of the Buddha: A Translation of the Dīgha Nikāya*, trans. Maurice Walshe (Somerville, Mass.: Wisdom Publications, 1995), 91.

3. See Ariyapariyesana Sutta, Majjhima Nikāya 26. *The Middle Length Discourses of the Buddha: A Translation of the Majjhima Nikāya*, trans., ed., and rev. Bhikkhu Ñāṇamoli and Bhikkhu Bodhi (Somerville, Mass.: Wisdom Publications, 1995), 253.

Chapter 4: Skillful Effort from First Sit to First Jhāna

1. Bhikkhu Ñāṇamoli, *The Life of the Buddha* (Kandy, Sri Lanka: Buddhist Publishing Society, 1998), 171.

2. Amy Schmidt, *Knee Deep in Grace: The Extraordinary Life and Teaching of Dipa Ma* (Lake Junaluska, N.C.: Present Perfect Books, 2003).

Chapter 5: Material Jhānas

1. Bhadantacariya Buddhaghosa, *Visuddhimagga: The Path of Purification*, trans. Bhikkhu Ñāṇamoli (Seattle, Wash.: BPS Pariyatti, 1999), 150.
2. Ibid., 268.

Epilogue

1. Gil Fronsdal, "Insight Meditation in the United States: Life, Liberty, and the Pursuit of Happiness," in *The Faces of Buddhism in America*, ed. Charles S. Prebish and Kenneth K. Tanaka, chapter 9 (Berkeley: University of California Press, 1998).

Bibliography

Bodhi, Bhikkhu, trans. *The Connected Discourses of the Buddha: A Translation of the Saṃyutta Nikāya.* Somerville, Mass.: Wisdom Publications, 2000.

Ñāṇamoli, Bhikkhu. *The Life of the Buddha.* Kandy, Sri Lanka: Buddhist Publishing Society, 1998.

———. *The Middle Length Discourses of the Buddha: A Translation of the Majjhima Nikāya.* Translated, edited, and revised by Bhikkhu Bodhi. Somerville, Mass.: Wisdom Publications, 1995.

Buddhaghosa, Bhadantacariya. *Visuddhimagga: The Path of Purification.* Translated by Bhikkhu Ñāṇamoli. Seattle, Wash.: BPS Pariyatti, 1999.

Chah, Ajahn and Jack Kornfield. *Food for the Heart: The Collected Teachings of Ajahn Chah.* Somerville, Mass.: Wisdom Publications, 2003.

Fronsdal, Gil. "Insight Meditation in the United States: Life, Liberty, and the Pursuit of Happiness." In *The Faces of Buddhism in America,* edited by Charles S. Prebish and Kenneth K. Tanaka, chapter 9. Berkeley: University of California Press, 1998.

Gunaratana, Mahathera Henepola. *The Jhānas in Theravada Buddhist Meditation.* Kandy, Sri Lanka: Buddhist Publication Society, 1988.

Sayadaw, Pa Auk Tawya. *Knowing and Seeing.* Kuala Lumpur, Malaysia: WAVE Publications, 2003 (no copyright).

Schmidt, Amy. *Knee Deep in Grace: The Extraordinary Life and Teaching of Dipa Ma.* Lake Junaluska, N.C.: Present Perfect Books, 2003.

Thanissaro Bhikkhu. "Pushing the Limits: Desire and Imagination in the Buddhist Path." Access to Insight (2006), www.accesstoinsight .org/lib/authors/thanissaro/pushinglimits.html.

Walpola, Sri Rahula. *What the Buddha Taught.* New York: Grove Press, 1959.

Walshe, Maurice, trans. *The Long Discourses of the Buddha: A Translation of the Dīgha Nikāya.* Somerville, Mass.: Wisdom Publications, 1995.

Index

absorption, 71–73. See also *jhāna*
absorption concentration, 27–29
absorptions, 7, 23
acceptance, 56
access concentration, 26–28
vs. absorption concentration,
29
Acinna. *See* Pa Auk Tawya Sayadaw
ānāpāna nimitta, 62, 117
draws awareness into first *jhāna,*
62–63
nimitta and *ānāpāna* spot becoming, 61–62
ānāpāna spot, 14–17, 21, 38, 39, 59
inability to feel breath at,
42–43
merging with *nimitta,* 61–62 (see
also *ānāpāna nimitta*)
ānāpānasati meditation practice, 12,
38, 119, 120
instructions, 14–16
air element, 120
anatta resolves, 44
attachments, 11
attainments, 30
chasing, 29–30, 33–34
attention. See *vicāra; vitakka*
attitude, 56
attractions and aversions, 8–9
aversion. *See* ill will/aversion

"base" meditation object, 97–98
base of boundless consciousness,
103–6
base of boundless space, 102–5
base of neither perception nor
nonperception, 108–11
base of nothingness, 106–8
bhavanga, checking, 76–78
with wisdom eye, 77, 91, 92, 96,
111–12
Bhikkhu, Thanissaro, 35–36
bliss. See *sukha*
bliss states, cultivating, 34
boundless consciousness, base of,
103–6
boundless space, base of, 102–5
breath (as meditation object), 12,
14–16, 21, 42–43
counting, 15
difficulties sensing/following,
42–43
Pa Auk on, 15, 16, 43
"whole breath body," 14, 16
Buddha (Siddhārtha Gautama),
1–4, 97
on doubt, 49
practiced *vipassanā* and *samatha,*
32
on proper tension in meditation, 57

FACING PAGE: *Venerable Pa Auk Sayadaw with Tina Rasmussen and Stephen Snyder at the Forest Refuge.*

About the Authors

STEPHEN SNYDER, after traveling through Asia as a youth, began practicing Buddhist meditation in 1976 at the age of nineteen. Since then he has had a daily meditation practice in addition to completing numerous retreats. Stephen is the first American male authorized to teach by the Venerable Pa Auk Sayadaw. He also works as a professional coach and lawyer.

TINA RASMUSSEN began meditating in 1976, at the age of thirteen. She was ordained as a Buddhist nun by the Venerable Pa Auk Sayadaw and is the first Western woman he authorized to teach. Tina has also worked as an organizational development consultant for more than twenty-five years and has received a PhD and published numerous business books.

Please visit their website at www.JhanasAdvice.com for further information and recommended resources.

© John Mercer